Mule Deer
Behavior, Ecology, Conservation

Text by Erwin A. Bauer
Photographs by Erwin and Peggy Bauer

Voyageur Press

Edited by Elizabeth Knight
Designed by Kathryn Mallien
Printed in China
96 97 98 99 5 4 3 2

Library of Congress Cataloging-in-Publication Data
Mule deer: behavior, ecology, conservation / text by Erwin A. Bauer ; photographs by Erwin and
Peggy Bauer
p. cm.
Includes bibliographical references and index.
ISBN 0-89658-263-9
1. Mule deer. I. Bauer, Peggy. II. Title.
QL737.U55B386   1995
599.73'57—dc20   94-39531
CIP

Distributed in Canada by Raincoast Books, 8680 Cambie Street, Vancouver, B.C. V6P 6M9

Published by Voyageur Press, Inc.
P.O. Box 338, 123 North Second Street, Stillwater, MN 55082 U.S.A.
612-430-2210, fax 612-430-2211

Please write or call, or stop by, for our free catalog of natural history publications. Our toll-free number to place an order or to obtain a free catalog is 800-888-WOLF (800-888-9653).

Educators, fundraisers, premium and gift buyers, publicists, and marketing managers: Looking for creative products and new sales ideas? Voyageur Press books are available at special discounts when purchased in quantities, and special editions can be created to your specifications. For details contact our marketing department.

Page 1: A late autumn sun illuminates a mule deer near Mammoth in Yellowstone Park.
Pages 2–3: A mule deer buck on the Great Plains. Muleys thrive where the land is not overgrazed by livestock.
Page 5: At the onset of the rut, this mule deer is traveling toward a traditional breeding area.

Dedication

This book is dedicated to all of the organizations, and their chapters and members, that are devoted to preserving, protecting, and restoring mule deer country in North America. This list includes the Sierra Club, the Boone and Crockett Club, the Wilderness Society, Defenders of Wildlife, the National Audubon Society, the Canadian Nature Federation, the National Wildlife Federation, the Greater Yellowstone Coalition, the Montana Wilderness Association, the Jackson Hole Alliance, the Wildlife Management Institute, the Rocky Mountain Elk Foundation, the Nature Conservancy, the Montana Environmental Information Center, and the National Parks and Conservation Association.

Contents

Facing page: A golden fall sun illuminates a grassland buck. He is watching a herd of does pass along a dry creek bed below.

The Mule Deer of the American West

"The ears and tail of this Animal when compared with those of the Common [meaning whitetailed] Deer, so well comported with those of the Mule when compared with the Horse, that we have by way of distinction adopted the appellation of Mule Deer."
—William Clark, The Journals of Lewis and Clark, March 11, 1806

During a lifetime spent outdoors, watching and photographing wildlife, I've found that some memories are especially vivid and lasting. One day in June in the early 1950s, wilderness guide Gene Wade and I saddled two riding horses, lashed light camping gear onto a pack horse, and from Cooke City, Montana, rode out into the Beartooth Mountains northeast of Yellowstone National Park. Our destination was remote Fossil Lake where the fishing for native cutthroat trout is always fast and furious as soon as the winter ice breaks up.

But this time we had miscalculated. We arrived saddlesore late in the day, only to find the lake still covered with a crust of ice. We pitched camp anyway and, after breakfast the next morning, decided to hike onward to another alpine lake that might have thawed. We hobbled the horses, stuffed fishing tackle in rucksacks, and headed up a steep game trail through that beautiful, still-primitive country.

A mile or so from our starting point, we saw a mule deer doe. There is nothing unusual about that, but this one seemed to follow us—and that is strange behavior. She seemed very nervous, agitated, and kept some distance above and behind us. Gene suggested we pause and sit down to see what would happen. The doe did not come any closer; instead she began to circle around above us and soon disappeared into a draw.

After resting quietly for about five minutes, we shrugged and reshouldered our rucksacks, preparing to move on. That's when I saw the spotted reddish brown fawn. It was bedded barely twenty feet (6 m) from where we had stopped, head flat on the ground, but large, dark eyes wide open and staring directly at us, probably in terror. Despite its color, the fawn was surprisingly well camouflaged in the early summer vegetation and did not move.

"Let's head on out," my companion said softly.

At that time, I was still living in Ohio, whitetailed deer country, but I was spending most summers in the Rocky Mountains, a pleasure that would in time become an addiction. I had encountered mule deer for the first time in Yellowstone Park in 1935 and have seen a good many since then. But meeting that anxious mother and the newly born fawn on a Beartooth alpine trail was one of several incidents that triggered an interest in the species that has only grown deeper over the years.

A photo of a beautiful buck such as this justifies making plenty of footprints up steep mountain trails. Muleys are normally not as nervous as whitetails, as is evident in this mellow mule deer buck.

Since then, my wife Peggy and I have focused cameras on everything from armadillos to zebras, from hyenas to penguins, on every continent, but many of our happiest, most exciting days have been spent photographing the mule deer of the American West from birth to death. Since 1971, we have lived on intimate terms in Wyoming, and then Montana, with *Odocoileus hemionus*, as mule deer are named by scientists. Fawns were born just beyond our bedroom window in Jackson Hole, where we lived for many years. Every fall a few mule deer wander down from their high summer range in the Absaroka-Beartooth Wilderness Area in Montana to spend the winter on our land that overlooks the upper Yellowstone River valley.

We have whitetailed deer wintering on the place, too. But while the whitetails remain shy and never seem to really trust us, the mule deer behave more like old friends. They interrupt their browsing to watch us hike up along Deep Creek and seldom waste as much energy racing away from us as do the whitetails. It is a pleasure to see them for they brighten a bitter January day, even when the sky is low and it is snowing hard.

From the Old to the New World

About fifteen million years ago an extraordinary migration of wild creatures began across the land bridge that once connected Siberia and Alaska during the later phases of the Ice Age, or the Pleistocene. It was most likely a gradual movement or shifting rather than a great, sudden surge. Among the countless creatures that plodded eastward from Asia to the New World were the ancestors of our elk, moose, caribou, and deer, followed eventually by the nomadic peoples that subsisted on them. The humans found a land already occupied with native species, and for a while, life amid the profusion may have been relatively easy, and the hunting was good.

In time, the last glaciers of the Ice Age would cover vast areas of North America, exterminating some unadaptable or less-competitive species. The ancestors of our deer somehow survived not only the ice, followed by periods of drought, but also a host of predators such as sabertoothed tigers, the ancestors of today's gray wolves, and of course the Stone Age human hunters. The sabertoothed tigers are gone, the wolves are going, and the humans today have inherited the whole earth. But two species of deer survived and evolved through that long period of drastic change.

When the Pilgrims from England waded ashore at Plymouth Rock nearly four centuries ago on the Atlantic Coast, and the Spanish soldier-missionaries colonized the Pacific Coast, they found the two deer living in greatly differing habitats. Whitetailed deer lurked in eastern forests on the Pilgrim side. Mule deer ranged over the mountains, plains, and badlands of the western one-half to two-thirds of our continent on the Spanish side. This book is about the mule deer, that tenacious survivor and a species that has enriched our lives.

Subspecies and Range

No common name is universally accepted for all the species of *Odocoileus hemionus*. In most of the American West, the animals are called mule deer, a name inspired by the large size of their ears, compared to those of whitetailed deer. In the Pacific Northwest, it was the tail that caught the eye of the namers, and there the animals are known as blacktailed deer.

Scientists and taxonomists now generally agree that there are seven distinct subspecies of mule and blacktailed deer in existence today. (The main differences are in certain skull and tooth measurements, although there is also subtle variation in body size and color.) The most familiar and widespread is *O.h. hemionus*, the Rocky Mountain "muley" whose range is several times larger than that of all the others combined. It lives from New Mexico northward to the top of Alberta and from Nevada eastward to western Nebraska. The heaviest mule deer ever hoisted onto honest scales was of this subspecies in British Columbia. It weighed 385 pounds (175 kg) field-dressed (with the body cavity cleaned), which means it would have carried almost a quarter-ton (225 kg) on the hoof. A mule buck half that size would be larger than average.

The California mule deer, *O.h. californicus*, lives in the High Sierra (or Sierra Nevada) and southern California. Usually its coat—grayish tan in winter and reddish brown in summer—is paler than the Rocky Mountain deer's pelage. But outwardly it differs mostly in its smaller (three-and-a-half-inch-long [9-cm-long]) metatarsal glands, compared to five inches (13 cm) in its cousin from the Rocky Mountains. The furtive Southern mule deer, *O.h. fuliginatus*, is found in the rough foothills and mountain spine of northern Baja California. The now very uncommon peninsula muley, *O.h. peninsulae*, clings to existence in the dry, brown landscape of southern Baja California. Southern Arizona, north-central Mexico, and West Texas are

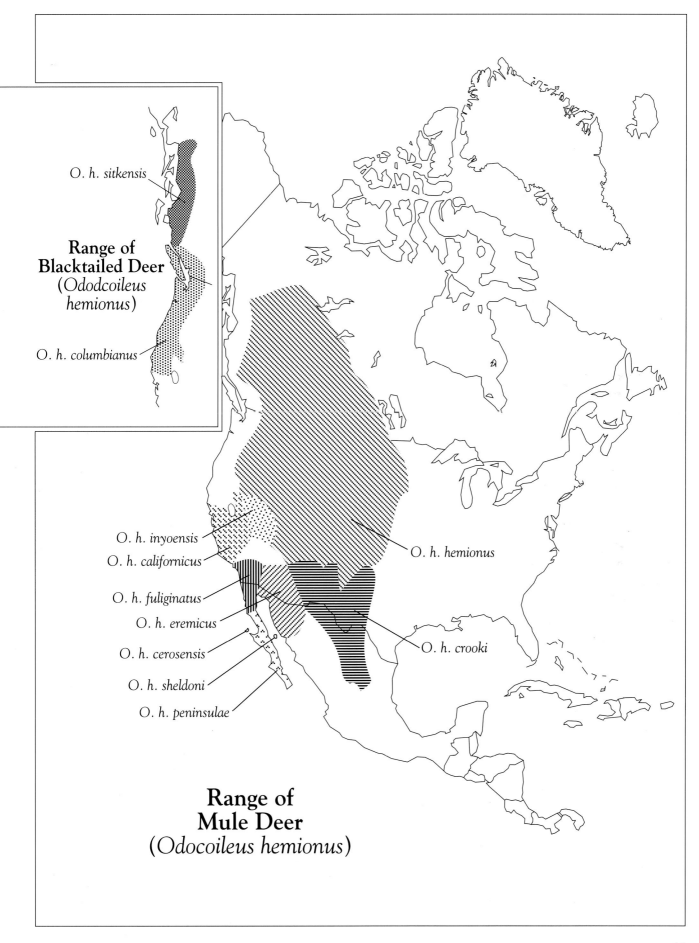

Range of
Blacktailed Deer
(*Ododcoileus
hemionus*)

O. h. sitkensis

O. h. columbianus

O. h. inyoensis

O. h. californicus

O. h. fuliginatus

O. h. eremicus

O. h. cerosensis

O. h. sheldoni

O. h. peninsulae

O. h. hemionus

O. h. crooki

**Range of
Mule Deer**
(*Odocoileus hemionus*)

the home of the slightly smaller (than the Rocky Mountain) desert mule deer, *O.h. crooki.*

The other two subspecies are much more commonly known as blacktailed deer than as mule deer, due to their dark-colored tails. The Columbian blacktail, *O.h. columbianus,* inhabits a narrow strip along the Pacific Coast from northern California to British Columbia. In California it also lives well inland in the Cascade Mountains. The damp, green coastal forests of southeastern Alaska support a good population, sometimes even a density, of reddish brown Sitka blacktails, *O.h. sitkensis.* Both blacktails will be covered in more detail in the chapter "Blacktailed Deer."

At one time, four other mule deer races or populations were considered as separate subspecies. But now the Tiburón Island and Cedros Island muleys and the burro and Inyo deer of California are regarded either as intergrades or as insufficiently different from the others to be listed separately.

Looking at a Mule Deer

The basic healthy mule deer is a sturdy, handsome mammal no matter how it is viewed. Only males grow antlers, the crowns that make deer so fascinating to people, although there are exceptions to this since every year hunters shoot a few does that show some antler growth. More detail about mule deer antlers is in the chapter "Antlers."

Pelage

All mule deer of the Rockies and other western mountains wear one of two coats depending on the season. The relatively short, reddish brown summer coat, which is worn for three or four months, has little underfur and is quite sleek. This pelage is shed in early fall and replaced by a much heavier, grayish tan winter coat under which curls a dense mat of fine hair. This is extremely good insulation as it must be in most of the species' range, where temperatures can fall to well below zero Fahrenheit (-18 degrees Celsius) and remain there for weeks. Males tend to be darker than females, and the coats of both appear bleached out at the end of winter.

The mule deer's tail is small, resembling a short length of heavy white rope with a black tip, which is rarely raised during flight. In all seasons, mule deer have white chin patches, white throats and bellies, and a white or light-colored rump patch.

Size and Weight

For five months following the fall rut, a mule deer fetus grows slowly inside the pregnant female. But then growth accelerates as the spring crop of new browse becomes available. The does separate from their wintering herds and retreat to secluded areas where in late May or, more often, early June, spotted fawns are born, weighing in the range of five to eleven pounds (2–5 kg).

Facing page: A Columbian blacktail in the velvet along the Oregon coast.

Facing page, top: An early snow falls in the northern Rocky Mountains. This alert buck, neck swollen, begins the search for does ready to breed. Facing page, bottom: Four does rest in the cold winds of an autumn snowstorm. Above: This buck has an antler spread even wider than his substantial mule deer ears. If you add the number of points and heavy beams, it is obvious you are looking at a fine trophy animal.

On good mule deer range the fawns grow quickly. By late fall, if it has been well nourished, a fawn following its mother may be very close to her size and weight.

The weights of adult mule deer vary greatly depending on the area in which they live and even on the season. But following are some average weights of bucks collected at a research station in eastern Wyoming: yearling males averaged 129 pounds (59 kg); two-year-olds averaged 170 pounds (77 kg); ages three to five averaged 206 pounds (94 kg); deer six years and older averaged 249 pounds (113 kg). Bucks put on the scales at a hunter checking station in southern Montana weighed pretty much the same as those in Wyoming. Alberta bucks may be somewhat heavier. Does weigh less than bucks of the same age living on the same range.

Like many of the larger mammals, mule deer are never as big as they seem. The backs of the biggest bucks I have examined closely would not have been much higher than my belt buckle (which, incidentally, is carved from a discarded mule deer antler). The bellies of few mule deer would clear the ground by more than two feet (61 cm).

Physique and Flight

The mule deer's physique is built on a light but strong skeleton, developed through natural selection over thousands of years. Evolution has produced a very swift, durable, and agile animal, able to outrun enemies most of the time. Its seemingly fragile outward appearance is deceptive. Not only is a mule deer able to disappear at astonishing speed, but it can do so over very rough ground, up or down steep slopes. In flight, it can also suddenly change direction, a maneuver that would seem to snap its thin front legs, or at least twist a knee. But this probably never happens. Time and again when hiking, backpacking, or photographing bighorn sheep in summertime in high country above the timberline, I have found mule deer bucks. They always seemed to me to be at least as comfortable in this rugged environment as the sheep, which many suppose are the only natural denizens of such places.

This fine muley buck in its prime, ready to jump and run, has wide-spread, handsome antlers.

Above: This large buck demonstrates unusual agility in descending a nearly vertical canyon wall to reach the stream below. Facing page: For the first few weeks of their lives, mule deer fawns are left alone by their mothers, who are away feeding. If found, these fawns should not be moved or touched. They have not been abandoned.

Mule deer walk and run on their "toes"—on their pointed hooves—rather than on flat feet as do most other mammals, and this also gives them an advantage when a situation calls for speed. Muleys may not be as swift as the pronghorns that often share their open, eastern range. They may not be able to leap as high as whitetailed deer. But they can bound noisily through a forest as rapidly as any other animal of similar size, and they can vanish as silently as a shadow.

Vision, Hearing, and Smell

Many studies examine how well mule deer see, hear, and smell. The conclusion is: *very* well on all three counts. But beyond that there is some disagreement. It is safe to say that any muley's vision is far better than a human's and is especially good at detecting motion. The animals can see perfectly well in the dark, at least well enough to run at top speed through dense cover, deftly avoiding collisions with trees or other obstacles.

The hearing of this species is keen enough not only to hear sounds of different pitches, but also to instantly catalog them. To a deer, the sound of an approaching human, or a bear, or a string of pack horses differs greatly from the sounds made by other deer. A doe browsing at the edge of a mountain meadow also knows immediately if the deer sounds she hears are from relaxed or nervous and frightened animals. She reacts accordingly.

Mule deer are not especially vocal animals. A fawn bleats when separated too far from its mother. Occasionally, does utter deep, coarse noises described as blatts, maybe when another deer browses too near. Both sexes snort when surprised or uncertain by blowing air out through the nose, but not as often as white-tails do.

Most disagreement about mule deer senses is over smell. It is far better than an average person can comprehend, but still may be less acute than, say, a bear's or a coyote's. But when information obtained through a deer's nose is combined in the brain with what it sees and hears, it certainly makes the animal very aware of the current situation.

A keen sense of smell enables deer to keep in touch with one another, especially mothers and fawns. Bucks are able to find and then follow does during the rut, or breeding season, by the lingering scent of urine or estrus in the air.

Intelligence

One characteristic of mule deer that cannot be as accurately measured as body weight or antler dimensions is their intelligence. Many who have studied them believe they are fairly "smart" animals, even able to "think." Others are convinced they are not especially bright and always behave on instinct alone. The disagreement is greatest among hunters, particularly when they debate which is the warier, or the greater, game species—the muley or the whitetail.

An Alberta mule deer buck drinks at dusk. In some dry parts of their range, mule deer can survive for days while drinking very little water.

How to Tell a Muley From a Whitetail

Because we live where both mule deer and whitetailed deer are common sights just beyond our back door, I often notice the differences between the two. The antler conformation of bucks differs, and I will discuss that in more detail in the chapter "Antlers." The tails also differ. A mule deer's tail is white, short, and ropelike with a dark spot on the end. The tail of a whitetailed deer is pennant- or spade-shaped, all white underneath and brown on top. The tails of blacktailed deer (a mule deer subspecies) are like those of whitetails, except that they are black on the outside. But despite nearly daily sightings, a long time passed before I realized that the metatarsal glands, those on the hind legs between hocks and hooves, are covered with brown hair on mule deer, but with white strands on whitetails.

Despite all of these distinctions, the most noticeable difference is in the way the two species run. Startle a whitetail, and it escapes in a fluid, flowing lope, punctuated by broad graceful leaps, that is truly beautiful to see. Flush a mule deer, and it stots, or bounds away in a unique, stiff-legged gait that seems almost kangaroolike. It appears to strike downward and backward with all four feet at once. That may seem awkward, but is ideal for rough terrain and is deceptively swift. A mule deer can easily cover twenty feet (6 m) or more in a bound. Take my word that it is very difficult to follow, with a camera and long telephoto lens, an animal traveling like that.

In addition, there is evidence, some of it debatable, that mule deer are becoming warier with time. More and more they seem to behave whitetails do in this respect. Blame it on increased hunting pressure, on the invasion of some mule deer country by whitetails, on the opening of ever larger areas of once-remote mule deer range, or on some combination of these factors. Once the conventional wisdom said that when alarmed, mule deer tried to put distance between themselves and the perceived danger, while whitetails tried to use cover to hide. Today, it seems to me, a lot of mule deer are using both cover and distance to survive.

Top: Whitetailed deer bound or gallop gracefully when alarmed. Running at full speed seems almost effortless. Bottom: In contrast to whitetails, mule deer seem to bounce, or stott, away on stiff legs. But they are fast afoot nonetheless.

Mule deer still run on the grasslands of the western Great Plains, but their numbers here are gradually decreasing. Overleaf: At daybreak in early autumn, two young bucks pause at the edge of a mountain lake. Both are nervous about being so exposed.

This much we do know: The brains of both the mule deer and the whitetail are smaller relative to body size and much smoother than a human brain. This indicates that deer are not nearly so wise as people or probably as some other animals that share their habitat. But a hunter who has found nothing but fresh deer tracks all day will find that hard to believe. A mule deer more than makes up for any intellectual deficiency in its wariness and its ability to instantly react to danger by making hoofprints in another direction.

I am convinced that mule deer, like most large mammals, are wary in direct ratio to how long and how hard they have been hunted. The mule deer in Yellowstone National Park (which have not been hunted for one hundred years), for example, pay little attention to the people who swarm through the park from spring through fall. But go just a short distance beyond park boundaries and the only muleys you are likely to see are those in the distance, a distance that is steadily increasing.

From Birth to Death

"I like to watch the long-eared mule deer on a high ridge,
outlined against the sky. All living creatures are my relatives. . . ."
—Lakota holy man John (Fire) Lame Deer

Late one exquisite summer evening, I sat high on a ridge of the National Bison Range and savored the western Montana scene far below. The yellow meadow, creased by the dark ribbon of Mission Creek, was dotted with a herd of forty or so grazing buffalo. Their long shadows trailed far behind them. Beyond the buffalo a lone coyote was mousing while keeping a safe distance from the herd. Scattered small bands of pronghorn, sometimes called antelope, also grazed leisurely over the landscape. Then a movement atop another high ridge to my right caught my eye, and I focused my binoculars there.

Two mule deer does were bedded, facing in opposite directions as if on sentry duty. Just beneath them three fawns gamboled in an open glade, softly lit by the setting sun. The fawns ran in circles, jumped, kicked, butted heads, and sniffed each other. One caught a playmate off-balance and, with a butt, sent it rolling down the slope. Then the three regrouped and began all over again. I watched this exhibition of their youthful high spirits until dusk when only the bison herd, now much farther away, remained in the last rays of the sun. Altogether it was an idyllic scene of wild America that is too fast eroding.

Spring, Summer, and the Young

On that evening in Montana, when I saw the fawns at play, I had watched something more than just a magnificent scene. I also had had a rare look at the behavior of mule deer young. Those gamboling fawns were developing the physical strength, skill, and coordination they would need to become powerful runners and accomplished escape artists throughout their lives. At the same time, they were sharpening their senses. At intervals throughout their play, the fawns would suddenly stop and for a few moments stare intently all around. Barely two months old, they were already alert for danger. Increasingly, biologists realize that the play of young mule deer (and most other mammals) is as crucial to their health and survival as is their nutrition or their heredity.

For a while after birth, which was probably in early June, the fawns had been left alone most of the time, seemingly deserted, to sprawl or crouch motionless, out of sight in secluded places while the mothers fed nearby. At intervals the does returned long enough to nurse, to stimulate defecation, and maybe to quickly groom their fawns. Then they drifted away again. Presumably the almost-odorless, still-weak, spotted fawns are safest from predators when still and hidden.

Left alone by mother, a restless mule deer fawn begins to explore its environment in northwest Montana. This is a dangerous period for the young fawns, when they are most vulnerable to predation.

First pregnancies ordinarily result in single fawns. After that twins are common, and we have seen does followed by triplet fawns.

In the normal course of events, fawns will later follow their mothers at all times, everywhere across their summer range, eventually joining up with other families to form small bands. Just the same, fawn mortality might be high during some years in some areas, depending on such factors as the weather (long, cold rains can be fatal), the quality of the range, the presence of domestic livestock (a definite minus), and of course the abundance or scarcity of such predators as cougars, bears, coyotes, wolverines, and golden eagles. I once saw a mother mule deer drive away the coyote that had discovered her fawn, but I cannot believe this is a common occurrence.

Above: Tentatively, meekly, a mule deer fawn follows its mother along a forest edge. Right: Fawns are born in remote places, often in lush mountain meadows—perhaps even near the same spot where the mother was born. Overleaf: A mule deer buck in Banff National Park, Canada, tirelessly pursues two does.

Throughout their range, most mule deer fawns are born in early June. These twins lick each other, but such mutual grooming at this age may not be common.

The Rutting Ritual

Mule deer bucks have developed several unusual reproduction strategies. Every breeding-age buck faces the same stiff competition to discover does, as soon as possible, that are entering estrus. Once such a doe is identified, the buck must stay with her relentlessly and keep her from wandering away until she is ready to breed. Bucks can also determine whether and probably how soon a doe will come into estrus by urine-testing.

Spend time in a busy rutting area and you will soon see this testing. Bucks are constantly pursuing, stimulating, and poking does with their noses, antlers, and feet until they urinate. Even bedded females are prodded until they stand up to urinate, which almost all do to avoid the harassment. In a behavior called lip-curling, or flehmen (named after the biologist who first described it), males are able to smell urine and actually taste any sign of oncoming estrus. For further confirmation, bucks may lick the ground, the snow, or the doe's rear end. If the odor—the message—is strong and positive, the buck will remain with that prospect, unless he is driven away by a stronger buck. If the scent is weak, the buck will keep searching, testing every doe he encounters. Since females are frequently tested this way, possibly for

Not even a terrible blizzard has cooled the ardor of this rutting buck, here sniffing the wind for does.

weeks in the fall, they must somehow ration their urine.

Once a buck has "locked" onto a good prospect, he follows closely behind, head held low, flicking his tongue, making soft noises that some scientists suspect may be an imitation of a fawn's distress call. He may be trying to arouse the doe's maternal instincts. All the while, the buck tries to guide the female into a patch of woods or other isolated spot far from other deer. In time this system of testing and posturing usually succeeds. After seeming to reject advances, the doe finally stands in readiness and a fairly quick mounting and mating takes place.

Although fawn mortality may locally be very high throughout their first summer, mostly from predation, biologists know that, except in isolated instances, this does not greatly affect the size and health of the deer herd from year to year.

By late summer, the fawns are no longer nursing. As summer blends into fall, the healthiest survivors are full grown, or nearly so, and are self-reliant. A few of the most precocious female fawns may even be able to breed in November, before they are a year old. At the same time the mother's protective instinct begins to fade, but her fawns usually continue to stay near her through the fall rutting season and until the following spring.

Autumn and Breeding

Peggy and I have spent countless days—some might say far too many days—watching mule deer through binoculars, spotting scopes, and the viewfinders of our cameras. The pursuit has taken us to some of the finest wild country left in our land. All of it has been interesting, and some of it even fascinating. But the most exciting times by far are those during the rutting or breeding season.

Throughout its range, the mule deer rut is an annual rite of blustery, raw November that may extend into even colder December. It is a dramatic time of action and aggression. The herds of does gradually funnel downward, sometimes pushed by foul weather and

Facing page: At the onset of the rut, mule deer bucks constantly curl their lips to smell and taste the air, locating does in estrus. This lip-curling is called flehmen. Above: It is the peak of the breeding season, and a buck tests—smells—a doe for some sign of estrus. Left: When does come into estrus in November, they are followed relentlessly by bucks. The dominant buck, which usually has the heaviest antlers, follows most closely.

Facing page, top: In a common ritual of the rutting season, a buck slashes at brush with its antlers. This may be a means of working off aggression. Facing page, bottom: It is early November and head-to-head battles break out between bucks, usually of equal or nearly equal size. The bucks fight to establish rank for breeding rights. Above: Rutting duels between bucks often result in injury. This buck has been blinded in one eye by an antler point.

heavy snow, from the high green pastures of summer (where the fawns played) to lower and lower elevations. On this winter range, they are concentrated and more accessible to bucks that migrate to these areas at the same time. They meet in what are traditional breeding sites. Strong instinct, plus the hind leg, metatarsal, and tarsal scent glands further activated by the rut, enable animals ready to breed to locate one another, even over long distances. As November days grow shorter and colder, estrus is triggered first in one doe and then in another, until it appears contagious. Males are attracted to them from far and near.

The duration of the breeding season varies from year to year, it seems to me, but for two to four weeks male mule deer are involved in a continual tournament to determine which animal or animals will prevail and impregnate the great majority of does. The bucks posture and strut, slash at bushes and shrubs with smooth, hard antlers, follow individual does, curl their lips, and actually taste the air (in a lip-curling behavior known as flehmen) for the scent of estrus. A few really powerful males seem able to attract and to assemble small clusters of females, which voluntarily stay near them. If the posturing and body language isn't enough to establish rank or dominance, bucks then resort to sharp, savage antler clashes to drive rivals away or to challenge larger bucks.

In a typical fight, bucks square off head to head and, in this position, lunge and push until one is clearly the stronger and the other breaks away. But if one animal slips, or loses footing, or is clearly outclassed and fails to keep antler contact, a rival may drive antlers into its body or even into its face.

Occasionally the attrition from combat is heavy. Antler tines sometimes snap and more often there is damage done to the eyes. We have seen a number of bucks blind in one eye. Losers can also suffer body punctures that in extreme cases can be fatal, and we noted one young buck with the side of its mouth torn open. Despite the toll and maybe even because of it, the best genetic traits of the winners, such as keen senses and a strong physique, are passed on from generation to generation.

In many parts of the United States and Canada, the mule deer hunting season begins before the rut. So inevitably some of the larger, stronger bucks will be taken by trophy hunters before they have an opportunity to compete and breed. This causes concern that antler size in deer herds may gradually deteriorate, and

some scientists agree that this is the case. Other biologists, however, dismiss the theory, and there is no solid evidence either way. Another concern is that enough males may not survive the hunting season, when mostly bucks are killed, to impregnate all of the receptive does. But this fear also does not seem to be substantiated by scientific evidence.

Several studies in the Rocky Mountains show that there are few unbred does by the end of the rutting season. More than 95 percent of all does will have fawns. A sex ratio of one buck per twelve or thirteen does is enough to ensure breeding success. In one controlled herd in Alberta, a single buck was known to have bred at least seventeen does, which bore twenty-eight fawns the following summer.

As with most other wild animals, mule deer have a built-in mechanism that nearly guarantees successful breeding: Both sexes have a powerful, perhaps overpowering, urge to reproduce. Even though the enthusiasm, or more likely the physical ability, of the most active, dominant bucks might wane toward the end of the rut, it has been noted that the fervor of the unmated female deer does not also fade. More than once late in the season, we have seen does aggressively following bucks, even trying to mount them as a not-too subtle suggestion.

All mule deer lose some of their normal caution and avoidance of humans during the rut, but it is most noticeable among bucks. For example, this is the only time of year when it is possible to approach some wary males within photographic range. You shoot all your pictures of the wild ones with heaviest antlers right now . . . or not at all.

Winter and Survival

Mule deer are able to survive extremes in cold and heat. In Yellowstone National Park they live through winters when the temperature may plunge to -40 degrees Fahrenheit (-40 degrees Celsius), and where six months later it may exceed 90 degrees Fahrenheit (32 degrees Celsius). Some researchers believe that the species needs mature forests both for shade in summer and protection from great wind chill in winter.

Over most of its range the mule deer rut or breeding season takes place during cold, sometimes snowy mid- to late November. Still it is the time of greatest, most frenzied activity for the species. Most if not all of the mature does are bred by a few of the finest, strongest males, as they will be each fall as long as they

Let it Snow, Let it Snow, Let it Snow

Mule deer occupy a range that is subject to foul weather, especially in late fall. Autumn is also the time of the all-important breeding season.

In late November 1994, we were photographing a typical mule deer herd in southern Alberta. It was the peak of the rut, and one heavy buck was busy driving other bucks away from the eight or nine does he had managed to isolate in an open forest near a lake shore. The weather was cool and bright and there were few dull moments.

Then one night the barometer hit rock bottom and a terrible blizzard struck. The temperature dropped to zero and violent wind blasted our deer herd with snow. At first light, the deer seemed stunned. We found all of them bedded close together, plastered white with snow. But the inertia didn't last long. Soon the buck was on its feet, shaking off the snow and checking all the does in the group for signs of oncoming estrus. As we watched through our viewfinders, we concluded that despite the weather, the annual rut was proceeding as normal.

Even one of the worst blizzards in a decade does not change the mule deer's lifestyle or calendar. But eventually it drove two dedicated photographers back to a warmer environment.

A dominant mule deer buck shows real stamina during the rut despite extremely foul weather conditions.

live. The breeding period is followed by the season of least activity, winter's Hunger Moon, when most mule deer simply try to survive until spring. Nourishing food is no longer abundant and becomes increasingly scarce as the days drag on. The animals move only as much as is necessary, conserving heat and energy.

Although mule does reassemble into their (probably) familiar herds following the rut for the duration of winter, there are strains within the society. Competition for the available food increases, and living together does not necessarily mean sharing equally. Savage fights, kicking out with hooves, explode and then end quickly. Weaker animals, including fawns, are the last to feed. The bucks, not having fed for several weeks, may have lost as much as 15 percent of their body weight, including all of the summer's accumulated fat, and seem to me to be too weakened to fight. Whereas the first month or so of life is most dangerous for fawns, the post-rut winter takes the heaviest toll on adult males. Some may starve. But all of the bucks are weakened from the rut and are, therefore, more

vulnerable to predators.

Unusually long periods of intense cold in winter can cause females to abort or reabsorb fetuses, especially if they are drained of energy from having to travel far for food. Winter recreation activities of humans, especially snowmobiling across deer winter range and other serious disturbances, can also cause does to enter the spring season without a fawn. Studies show that mule deer burn up to six times as many calories walking through knee-deep snow as they do on bare ground, so forcing them to run through drifts is extremely detrimental to the deer's survival chances.

The most bitter and snowy winters may even drive mule deer into mountain towns to forage. During the late 1980s for example, deer began moving into Jackson, Wyoming. At first the townspeople regarded them as a pleasant novelty, but then the deer began to browse ornamental shrubbery down below the snow line. Some well-meaning citizens put out bales of hay for the hungry deer, against the advice of the Wyoming Fish & Game Department. By that time, the animals

Left: As the rut winds down, tired mule deer bucks seem to lose interest and rest more. They may have lost as much as 15 percent of their body weight including most of the fat acquired in the fall. It is not unusual to find a buck completely exhausted after breeding season. Above: This doe, as all others, now faces the long cold winter when food is scarce and starvation looms.

were in such bad condition that they were unable to derive any nutrition from the hay, and some died with full stomachs. In addition, the toll from bands of unrestrained dogs and road kills was very high. Mule deer are much better off outside any city limits, no matter how desperate the winter.

To Eat, To Prosper

One of the first things a serious mule deer watcher discovers is that while muleys are primarily browsers, they are not exclusively so. It seems to me that mule deer at least sample almost all of the plants at some state of growth in a given habitat. Multiply that by the number of different habitats they frequent in North America, and you have a list of foods longer than anyone has yet compiled. In summer, for example, a Rocky Mountain deer herd will wander, browsing, over alpine meadows, from aspen groves into evergreen forests, occasionally above timberline into areas of tundra. Mule deer winter ranges are likely even more varied, from juniper canyon bottoms and sagebrush foothills to arid scrub ranchlands and irrigated alfalfa or crop fields. One catalog of foods eaten by Rocky Mountain deer listed 788 different plant species. More than half of these were forbs; a quarter were trees and shrubs; the rest consisted of grasses and sedges.

There are some plants mule deer cannot pass up at least some of the time. The list would include chokecherry, wild rose, bitterbrush, young quaking aspen, snowberry, serviceberry, willow, and buffalo berry. Some favorite forbs are cinquefoil, fleabane, phlox, lupine, aster, buckwheat, and beardtongue. Bluegrass, fescue, and wheatgrass are consumed. Many, if not most, of these plants and grasses are eaten only at certain times, presumably at the peak of their nutritious content. So are some varieties of mushrooms. Calcium is the one element that appears most regularly in foods mule deer prefer. Sodium, which also can be obtained at natural mineral licks, also seems important.

It is hard to determine exactly how much food mule deer need for good health, but it has been estimated that an adult requires about two pounds of food per one hundred pounds (1 kg per 45 kg) of body weight each day just to survive average winter conditions. In spring and summer when there is an abundance of food full of nutrients, mule deer, like other creatures, gorge on them.

I should include here some important new information about mule deer health and survival. It has long been conventional wisdom that the fresh browse that grows following the clear-cutting of old growth forest, so excessive and widespread across the western United States and Canada, is a boon for mule deer, particularly in winter. But Montana State University deer biologist Richard J. Mackie now claims that's untrue. He has learned that the new growth browse is far less nutritious than that in the original old growth forests. He also believes that given adequate browse, muleys are able to withstand extremes of heat and cold far better than we previously realized.

That mistake about new versus old growth forest, Mackie points out, is based on our common knowledge of whitetailed deer experience. Whitetails certainly do thrive on cutover woodlands. But not only do mule deer fail to prosper on new growth, but they are generally not as adaptable as whitetails in other respects. Whitetails are able to live almost anywhere, even in suburbs and city parks. When human development encroaches on their habitat, they just eat the landscaping plants and new lawns, while mule deer are totally displaced. This new information should cause the planners and managers of our public and private land in the West not to allow development where it will be harmful to mule deer. They must also curtail the timber harvest, not only for the mule deer, but for the quality of the environment we all share.

Facing page, top: Even as the rutting season comes to a close, the drive to breed is not completely gone. A weary buck may still remain alert for females in estrus, as this mule deer shows. Facing page, bottom: To save energy after a heavy snowfall, does follow one another in search of food.

The Beauty of Mule Deer Digestion

Like all cloven-hoofed mammals, the mule deer is both browser, feeding on trees, shrubs, and bushes, and grazer, eating grasses. Due to the mule deer's herbivorous diet, it has a large liver and protein-rich saliva but does not have a gall bladder. The mule deer is a ruminant, which means it has a four-chambered stomach that has been described as a handy eat-now, digest-later body organ.

It is a sunny morning in September, every mule deer's last chance to really gorge on green vegetation before the rut begins and the snow falls.

Here's how mule deer digestion works. Mouthfuls or small bites of leaves, twigs, buds, shoots, or berries are swallowed with a minimum of chewing. The rough material goes into a rumen, which is simply a storage area somewhat like the crop of a bird. Bacteria and other micro-organisms break down the plant cellulose and start digestion. Later, at leisure, the partly processed food is regurgitated, bit by bit, as cud, chewed much more thoroughly, and swallowed again, this time bypassing the rumen and continuing through the other chambers of the stomach. The beauty of this kind of digestive system is that the ruminants can consume large amounts of food quickly and then, in a safer, less exposed area, digest while resting. Some scientists today believe that this capability is one subtle reason mule deer and other cud-chewers are surviving so much better than such nonruminants as rhinos, tapirs, and wild horses, which are rapidly traveling toward extinction.

Left: This buck is preparing for the November-long pursuit of romance, feeding on the fruit and leaves of a chokecherry tree.

Blacktailed Deer

"A fine specimen of a blacktailed deer went bounding past camp this morning. A buck with wide spread of antlers, showing admirable vigor and grace. . . . Every movement and posture is graceful, the very poetry of manners and motion. . . . "
—*From* **My First Summer in the Sierra** *by John Muir*

Blacktailed deer have contributed many rich memories and a single chilling one to my life as a photographer. I recall a time on Alaska's Afognak Island when a summer storm had washed ashore the huge, decaying carcass of a Steller's sea lion. It rested, stinking, on a gravel beach just above the high tide line. Certain that the bonanza would soon attract brown bears, I built a photo blind of bleached driftwood and sat inside waiting for the action I hoped would soon come. I focused my camera at a spot past the sea lion where I expected my star actor to first appear.

A cold drizzle was falling when the first creature to find the carrion arrived. It was a bald eagle. Soon a fox was also scavenging on the scene, but both were too small to make an image large enough in my camera viewfinder. I wanted bigger game. Then I heard and saw from the corner of my eye the movement of something much larger in the brush directly *behind* me. I felt a cold chill all over. Suddenly I realized that I was trapped directly between a brown bear and its next meal.

Fortunately the "bear" turned out to be two young Sitka blacktail bucks with small antlers still in velvet. When eventually my pulse was back to normal, and with plenty of time to kill, I tried an old Tlingit (Indian) trick. Lacking the traditional alder leaf, I blew on a thin strip of plastic from a film wrapper held between two pieces of wood to make a squeal. The result was nothing like the bleat of a blacktail deer fawn I'd heard before, but that didn't bother the twin bucks who were about fifty yards (46 m) away. Immediately they came trotting directly toward my blind until one was looking down at me inside. What they saw was enough to send them stotting at full speed in the general direction of Siberia.

What always troubled me was that I did not get a single good picture of the approaching deer. Nor did a bear ever show up to dine on the sea lion.

Columbian Blacktailed Deer

There are two races or subspecies commonly called blacktailed deer, the Columbian and the Sitka. Today the Columbian subspecies occupies the coastal range from California northward to southern British Columbia and inland to the Cascade and Sierra mountain ranges.

A Columbian blacktail buck in velvet pauses before flight into the deep evergreen forest.

Appearance and Behavior

At first glance, a Columbian blacktail looks and behaves like a composite of a whitetail and a mule deer. It has the pennant-shaped tail of the former, but this tail is all black instead of brown on the outside. Its antlers and ears, however, are like those of the mule deer.

When frightened sufficiently to flush, a blacktail bounds away, usually uphill, in the same stiff-legged, stotting gait of other mule deer. That seems to work very well in the mossy, evergreen northwestern forests that are usually littered with deadfalls and stumps from past logging. Stotting also allows a deer to suddenly change direction and to escape such predators as cougars.

But I have long noticed another trait of blacktails. Especially if the ground cover is very dense, some are inclined to skulk—to lie or stand motionless as whitetails sometimes do, rather than bolt immediately when danger approaches. During such a delay, some primitive intelligence may be deciding whether to flee, and if so, in what direction. It has been noted that compared to carnivores, all deer are slow learners. But as the deer become increasingly accustomed to people and their pets, the learning curve just may be rising, as evidenced by the widespread hunters' belief that they are harder and harder to tag.

Seasons of the Columbian

All deer are prolific creatures, and Columbian blacktails are no exception. Every doe in a herd of twenty or so will be impregnated as long as there is a single mature male available. Seven months later, to coincide with the May or June peak of new green growth of browse plants, the fawns are born. For a few weeks to a month or more, blacktail fawns primarily hide (as do other mule deer young) while their mothers feed. Fewer than half will survive predation and other hazards to reach maturity. In densely populated blacktail country, family dogs running without restraint take a far heavier toll every year than their owners are willing to admit. In northwestern Washington, dog predation has become a very serious matter. In addition, road kills along the expanding, high-speed highway system damage the population.

High on Hurricane Ridge in Washington's Olympic National Park, a Columbian doe crosses a lupine meadow.

Facing page: Typical antler formation on a Columbian blacktail buck. Blacktail antlers average much smaller than those of Rocky Mountain mule deer of the same age. Above: A beam of sunlight penetrates the dense forest canopy and spotlights a typical Columbian blacktail buck in velvet.

The Past and the Future

Early in the nineteenth century, as the explorers Lewis and Clark drifted slowly down the Columbia River toward their destination, the Pacific Ocean, they counted very few deer. Elk suspiciously watched the party pass downstream through the lush riverside meadows. But only scouting and hunting parties venturing inland ever saw many deer. The men were no doubt more interested in elk, which were larger than deer with more meat. But boaters making the same trip today would find the scenario reversed. Plenty of deer might be in sight, but few elk.

During the past century and a half, humans have drastically changed the lower Columbia Basin—in fact the entire Northwest—from a dense green virgin wilderness to a place where millions of people now lead an abundant life. Waves of new arrivals felled whole forests, cleared fields, built cities and subdivisions that never seem to end. This soon devastated many native wildlife species and changed the entire ecology of the region. For a long time, Columbian blacktailed deer alone seemed to benefit. "Opening up" the land and eliminating deer predators allowed this race of mule deer to increase to its greatest population ever. Peak numbers were reached in the 1950s or 1960s. This explosion of blacktail numbers in the Northwest can be

Heads and Tails

The antlers of mature mule and blacktail bucks are easy to distinguish from those of whitetail bucks of similar age. All of the tines or points of a whitetail's rack grow out of the two main antler beams. But the main beams of muleys and blacktails fork, and then each forks again as in the illustration. Mule deer antlers tend to be larger, in all dimensions, than blacktail antlers, which almost never spread, or extend, outward beyond the ear tips.

The white rump of a whitetail deer is mostly hidden by a pennant-shaped tail that is brown on the outside, but resembles a waving, white flag when raised. Mule deer tails are much smaller and, except for the black tips, are as white as the rump patch. In shape, the tail of a blacktail is somewhat similar to but smaller than a whitetail's. It is black on the outside and white underneath.

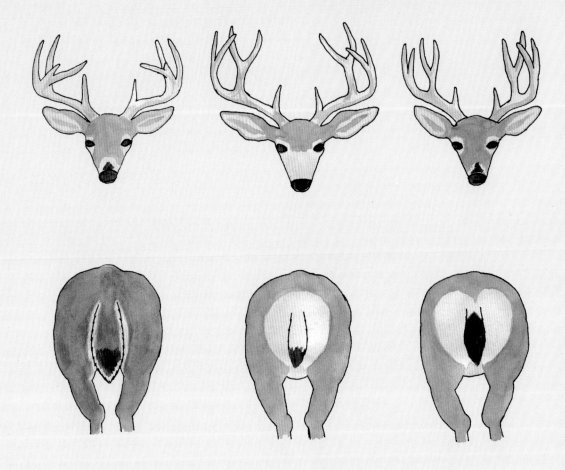

A comparison of the antlers and tails of whitetailed deer (left), mule deer (center), and blacktailed deer (right).

Facing page, top: Twin Columbian fawns in the lush, green forests of Mount Rainier National Park. Washington's Cascade Range has a fairly high abundance of blacktails. Facing page, bottom left: Blacktailed bucks, still in velvet, associate with and tolerate one another until the fall rut begins. Facing page, bottom right: A young and quite uncommon piebald Columbian blacktail on a private Washington sanctuary.

compared to the history of whitetails in the East, which multiplied so rapidly when lands east of the Mississippi River were converted from forests to farms.

Now in the 1990s, the diversified environment of the Northwest remains fairly favorable for blacktails. Some lumbering operations, human suburban settlements, and even forest fires and volcanic activity (as at Mount Saint Helens in Washington) have provided open areas and subsequent growth of plants on which to browse. Almost always nearby are deep woods for safety from enemies and shelter in severe winters. The density was estimated at between one and a half and two million in April of 1994, before the new crop of fawns was born.

In some areas where forage is plentiful, Columbians reach a density of 150 per square mile (60 per sq. km); this is both good and bad news. Biologists doubt that more than ten blacktails per square mile (4 per sq. km) could have lived in the towering pristine forests that impressed Lewis and Clark. Most believe that the density in the 1990s is not best for the environment, in the long run. The increase in human activity may now have tipped the balance in the other direction, one that is increasingly unfavorable to the Columbians.

Recent studies have concluded that blacktails prosper most when only about a third of any northwestern forest has been opened up. But in very few areas today is enough mature forest, or even *any* mature growth, left standing. Nor are there signs that our hunger for wood products, country homes, and lawns with gardens is slowing. Keep in mind also that it takes at least two centuries to grow a mature forest, and a good case has been made for the hypothesis that such old growth can never be duplicated.

So while they are numerous now, and no one worries about them, the future of Columbian blacktails isn't exactly bright. California game managers figure there were half as many Columbians in the Golden State in 1992 as there were in the 1960s. Numbers are dwindling in Washington, but there is only a slight downturn so far (the mid-1990s) in Oregon.

This Columbian blacktail doe is spending summer in the high mountain pastures of Olympic National Park, Washington.

Brown Bears and Blacktails

Anyone who wanders in Sitka blacktail country in a serious search for this subspecies is almost certain to also meet Alaskan brown bears, or at least see their signs, since the deer and bears share the same areas. Strange as it may seem, the deer somewhat depend on the bruins.

The vegetation along the Alaskan coastal zone is dense, and nearly impenetrable, thanks to the copious, almost year-round rainfall. The best, and often the only, way for deer to move through this wilderness is to follow bear trails. Grizzlies, as brown bears are also known, walk on traditional pathways, even placing their feet in the same spots time after time. The result is an obvious forest "highway." The blacktails amble along this route while browsing heavily on the plants easily accessible on each side. In time this use would lead to overbrowsing if it weren't for another activity of the brown bears.

All bears have prodigious appetites, especially in the weeks just before hibernation. Even a small one can eat eighty to ninety pounds (36–41 kg) of ripening wild berries and berry bushes every day. But what goes in one end quickly comes out the other. The short digestive tracts of bears do very little damage to berries and seeds, which often emerge intact. So each pile of bear scat contains both seeds and fertilizer and grows the next spring into a flourishing miniature garden, reestablishing plants that the deer might otherwise obliterate. By simply eating, walking on familiar trails, and defecating, the brown bears continually modify the landscape in favor of the deer. Occasionally in spring a brownie might catch a blacktail fawn in partial repayment.

Alaskan brown bears share almost all of Sitka blacktail range. In fact, the deer travel through dense forests on trails left by both brown and black bears and otherwise depend on their large neighbors.

A foggy, damp coastal forest near Sitka in southeastern Alaska. This is Sitka blacktail country.

Sitka Blacktailed Deer

The other and very similar blacktailed deer, the Sitka, is a native of the wet, coastal rain forests of southeastern Alaska and northwestern British Columbia. Its original range was limited but has been expanded by transplants to southeastern Alaska in the Yakutat area, to Prince William Sound, and to both Kodiak and Afognak Islands. This race seems to be thriving everywhere that vast areas of mature coastal forest have not been clear cut.

Appearance

The Sitka is a smaller, stockier subspecies than the Columbian blacktail or any of the other mule deer. It also has a noticeably shorter face. Fawns average about seven pounds (3.2 kg) at birth. The average live weight of adults in the fall is about 100 pounds (45 kg) for does and 150 pounds (68 kg) at most for bucks. The heaviest weight for a Sitka ever recorded was for an Alaskan buck that weighed 212 pounds (96 kg), field dressed (that is, with the body cavity emptied). It probably exceeded 250 pounds (114 kg) on the hoof and was a genuine giant for the subspecies.

In summertime a Sitka's coat is reddish brown, and by late fall it is replaced by a dark gray one. The antlers are small, usually very dark, with the typical blacktail branching of five points (including the eye guard) on each side. The Sitka shares this characteristic with the Columbian blacktail. Maximum antler growth is achieved by most bucks at four and a half to five and a half years of age. Life span rarely reaches six years, but one Alaskan animal was determined from its worn teeth to have lived to twelve.

Seasons of the Sitka

Sitka spotted fawns are born in May or June, often near forest edges, close to lowland muskeg, or even near ocean beaches. Before moving to summer range, the blacktails stoke up on new green beach grasses, sedges, and plantain. Then, following familiar trails on their upward migration toward open alpine country, they heavily utilize emerging skunk cabbage, marsh marigold, salmonberry, and blueberry leaves, all important foods. July finds the herds in high places, where deer cabbage is a favorite among the plenty of nutritious herbaceous plants.

Left: A Sitka blacktail of Afognak Island, Alaska. Top: Alaskan wild iris, such as this flower along the McNeil River, are common in Sitka blacktail country. Bottom: Columbian blacktails with velvet antlers in a typical environment. Blacktails seem more comfortable along the edges of uncut, mature forests.

Facing page: Normal high summer range of Sitka blacktailed deer in the coastal mountains of southeastern Alaska, a range shared with black and brown bears. Above: A Sitka blacktail buck stands alert in the coastal forests of southeastern Alaska.

The first heavy snows or frosts of autumn drive the deer down again into the shelter of tall timber. The rut takes place from late October to mid-November. As with all mule deer, Sitka bucks are so busy during the breeding season that they usually begin winter with the fat reserves of summer entirely depleted.

When salmon fishing or photographing seabirds with my friend Roy Randall, from his snug wilderness lodge at Seal Bay, Afognak Island, Alaska, I have more than once found deer swimming the cold, swift currents that separate Afognak from small satellite islands. They are surprisingly strong and apparently willing swimmers. Roy and I often debated whether the deer hit the water in search of better foraging or whether the bucks were just searching for romance at the beginning of the rut.

Alaskan coastal winters can be grim or fairly mild, sometimes both during the same year or even the same weekend. Studies show that most deer remain near, but below, the snow line, moving up and down to find forage. During times of very deep, wet snow, almost the entire Sitka population might be concentrated in a narrow zone along the coastal beaches.

Sitka deer are easiest to see when the belly-deep snows of winter or the failure of the berry crop inland drives them from evergreen cover to the open beaches. At such times they have little to feed upon but dry beach grasses and kelp. But the quality (nutrition) of these is low, and the deer have been known to starve at the edge of tidewater with full stomachs. Blacktails have also been observed eating dead fish that washed ashore from commercial fishing nets. This may be an act of desperation, a good source of energy, or both.

The Elusive Blacktail

Perhaps because blacktails are not regarded as highly by trophy hunters, or maybe because they are more furtive and therefore more difficult to study, our knowledge of them is less than that of the other North American deer. Years ago we met a disgruntled graduate student in British Columbia who had spent the previous two years researching the blacktail.

"What have you learned?" we asked.

"Not nearly enough," he admitted. He then explained how he had to devote too much of his time looking for his subjects in dense habitat where even dinosaurs would be hard to find. I understood his problem. Blacktails are as tough for photographers to approach as they are for biologists.

Antlers

"To be beautiful and calm, without mental fear, is the ideal of nature."
—From **The Life of the Fields** *by English naturalist and novelist Richard Jeffries*

One characteristic that distinguishes the deer of the world from all other animals is the growth of antlers on males. Every year new antlers grow (on all but two deer species) and several months later are discarded. Although far from the largest, the antlers of muleys are certainly among the most handsome and impressive of the Cervidae (deer) family. A fully mature, healthy mule deer buck of the northern Rocky Mountains, with antler growth at its peak, is always a majestic sight.

Like all other antlers, those of muleys are pure bone. These antlers grow outward from the base, like the branches of a tree, for seventeen to eighteen weeks in the summer. Mule deer antlers are often and incorrectly called deer horns, but horns are composed of a material called keratin (also found in animals' hooves and claws and in our finger- and toenails), rather than of bone, and are not shed every year. Bison, bighorn sheep, goats, and antelope, which share mule deer range, have horns. (Of these, the antelope is unique in that only the outer sheath of its permanent horns are shed annually.) Not only is deer antler pure bone, but it is also the fastest bone growth known.

Starting with Pedicles

Every deer's antlers grow out of pedicles, sometimes called "antler buds"—permanent twin stumps on the skull between the ears. Pedicles are the connectors between skull and antler bone. Although already faintly detectable on the heads of male mule deer even before they are born, the pedicles are visible only as cowlicks in the forehead hairs of buck fawns during their first year of life. It is extremely important for a fawn to have ample, rich nutrition available from the start, even while still a fetus in its mother's womb, because this will determine the size of its pedicles. Undernourished fawns of undernourished mothers have smaller than average pedicles. The best-fed does produce healthier fawns with larger than average pedicles.

But why is pedicle size important? All future antler growth depends on it. For example, a fawn born with small pedicles can never grow antlers larger than a certain modest size regardless of the quality of its food. But a fawn born at the same time with larger pedicles, from a combination of high-quality maternal nutrition and heredity, has the potential to grow larger and larger antlers as it matures.

With its high, heavy, symmetrical antlers, this powerful animal is ready to begin the rut as the dominant male in its area.

Above: The antlers of this buck appear to have been distorted by injury. But it could be that the animal simply is well past its prime. Right: A "cactus buck." An injury probably caused this buck in New Mexico to grow antlers with many points in a strange shape. The buck also did not shed its velvet before the onset of winter. Facing page: Weighing well over two hundred pounds, this old, heavy-bodied Alberta buck carries a fine rack of antlers.

The magnificent antlered mule buck you meet one autumn day on a wilderness trail or in a national park is a result of good breeding and good nutrition. And every set of antlers that qualifies for listing in the Boone and Crockett Club's *Records of North American Big Game* has a similar history. The mother was a healthy doe living on good range, providing an abundant variety of nutritious browse plants, especially during winter and early spring. The father was a powerful and dominant buck in the territory, equipped with heavy antlers. The record-book deer itself lived year-round on range not overpopulated by mule deer or elk and not overgrazed (or grazed at all) by livestock. Wise and serious trophy hunters, as well as naturalists and photographers, keep this last fact especially in mind when they go afield in the fall.

Growth and Development

A buck's antler tips first appear in the spring when it is about one year old. This is triggered by the increasing amount of daylight. During the next three to four months, growth will be slow, resulting in only spikes (or single tines) or forked antlers by autumn. Most nutrition during this first year of life is channeled into development of the skeleton and hence the body size. The spiked or forked antlers are shed in the fall. Each subsequent year, the deer grows and sheds increasingly larger racks of antlers, until maturity at about five and a half or six and a half years of age. From that time onward, as a process of natural aging, the size of the antlers slowly diminishes and may eventually assume a somewhat odd shape.

Throughout their growth and development, antlers are living appendages. They can be injured just as a leg can be fractured or a rib broken, causing a deformity or halting further growth. An interesting fact is that an injury to a buck's leg can be associated with a stunting or abnormal growth in the antler on the opposite side. Numerous blood vessels inside every antler supply blood and allow steady growth throughout the summer. In addition, during this time the antlers are covered with a vascular, sensitive skin coated with fine brown hair, called velvet. It is soft and warm to the touch. Mule bucks are "in the velvet" all summer

A Rocky Mountain mule deer in Alberta carries the start of a handsome antler rack, which sprouted in part from eating great amounts of summer's green bounty. The velvet on the antlers contrasts with his reddish summer coat.

Record Racks

Where in North America do mule deer grow the largest, heaviest antlers? According to the tenth edition (1993) of the Boone and Crockett Club's *Records of North American Big Game*, the largest typical rack with symmetrical opposing antlers belonged to an animal taken in Dolores County, Colorado, in 1972. It had six points on one side, five on the other. The second largest, taken in Hoback Canyon, Wyoming, can be seen in the Jackson Hole Museum. A most significant statistic is that almost half of all the largest mule deer racks recognized by Boone and Crockett came from one state,

A large mule deer buck in Waterton Lakes National Park, Alberta.

Colorado. However, the largest nontypical (nonsymmetrical) head, as well as the largest mass of mule deer antler known, was taken near Chip Lake, Alberta, in 1926. This rack had forty-three antler points and is said to have weighed about thirty pounds (14 kg). The odds of a larger muley rack ever occurring are very small.

Humans have always been fascinated by antlers and hunters have gone to great extremes to obtain the largest, especially those of North American deer. There is much more detailed information on all our native deer and their racks in our book, *Antlers*, published by Voyageur Press.

---

long and are very careful to avoid injury to their developing antlers. They do not use the velvet antlers to spar or to defend themselves.

By late summer or early fall, antler development slows, and a burr, or ring of bone, forms at the junction of the antler and the pedicle. Soon this burr chokes off the flow of blood, and antler growth stops. Either the velvet dries and peels off, or the buck rubs it off against a handy piece of vegetation. The antlers are now fully formed, hard, and dead. Often for a very brief time the newly peeled antlers are bright red with a coating of blood from the newly discarded velvet. But the blood soon oxidizes to a brown color. Peggy and I have photographed small bands of bachelor bucks in early fall when the red antlers of a single buck appeared unreal among the brown of its companions.

Once the antlers have peeled and hardened, they are no longer sensitive. Now for the first time a buck can use this branched "weapon" aggressively, first slashing at small trees and shrubbery and later sparring with rivals. The crash and rattle of antlers can be heard from far away during the rutting season. Then seven or eight months after the tips first appeared, and not long after the rutting season is over, the antlers are shed on a cold winter's day. Both may fall off on the same day and in nearly the same place, or they may be cast at

an interval of a week or so. In early winter in Montana, I have often seen mule bucks still wearing only one antler. Far less often have I found the two symmetrical antlers of a buck discarded in the same vicinity.

Why Do Deer Have Antlers?

Two questions invariably arise among scientists and in deer hunting camps, or wherever there is serious discussion about deer. Why do mule deer—in fact any deer—grow antlers? And, why do they shed and replace them each year?

One common theory for the shedding and replacement is that this process enables the buck's antler size to keep pace with its body growth. Another theory is that it allows replacement of antler tines snapped off in combat. While I have photographed mule deer with antler points missing and once or twice with an entire antler broken off, it is not very common. The true reason for annual shedding is probably still a mystery.

Also mysterious, many scientists say, is why deer have antlers at all. "For defensive purposes," seems an obvious answer. But mule bucks do not have their antlers throughout the winter when they are most needed to defend against predators. Also, when attacks on antlered bucks by unfettered domestic dogs, and on rare

Above: This buck has an unusually high rack. Before the rut, this impressive mule deer weighed at least 250 pounds. Left: This fine Rocky Mountain buck has just shed the velvet from its antlers, now stained with blood. The red will soon darken to brown.

The Boone and Crockett Club

In 1887, future president Theodore Roosevelt invited a number of America's best known big game hunters, naturalists, and conservationists to his home at Sagamore Hill. Few details of the meeting survive, but those present discussed many subjects: hunting ethics, game preservation, travel, vanishing species, and a unified wildlife conservation program for the nation. The meeting led to the formation that same year of the Boone and Crockett Club, America's first national conservation organization.

Over the years, many, if not most, of America's leading conservationists belonged to and were active in the Boone and Crockett Club, including George Bird Grinnell, Henry F. Osborn, George Shiras III, Stephen Mather, Horace Albright, Gifford Pinchot, Aldo Leopold, Ding Darling, and Charles Sheldon. The club was active in the establishment of Glacier and Denali National Parks, the National Forest System, the National Wildlife Refuge system and, in general, a fresh approach to wildlife conservation.

Although all native wildlife benefited and some threatened species were retrieved from the brink of extinction by Boone and Crockett influence, the mule deer is one species that may have benefited more than the rest. Much of the wilderness preserved by the organization's efforts was in the American West, mule deer country.

Headquartered today in Missoula, Montana, the Boone and Crockett Club displays its National Collection of trophy horns and antlers at the Buffalo Bill Historical Center in Cody, Wyoming. The largest known Sitka blacktailed deer head is on display there among many other world and near world records.

A heavily antlered Alberta buck rests very briefly during the rut. Minutes after this photo was taken, he was on his feet in pursuit of a doe.

Above: Muley bucks, too young to compete with older, stronger males during the annual rut, spar as a test of strength and to practice for future bouts. Facing page: This side view of an eight-point (four points per side) mule deer buck shows how the antlers of this species are normally branched.

occasions by wolves, have been observed, the deer defend themselves by striking out with their front hooves, not using their antlers at all.

A more likely theory is that deer have antlers both to challenge and defend themselves from rival bucks during the rut. We have often seen antlers used both ways. Savage, noisy combat does take place during the breeding season, and there are casualties. We have found mule bucks in late fall with flanks punctured and with eyes almost torn from the sockets in head-to-head fighting. In our experience, most of the antler sparring is done by medium to small males with others of similar size.

The main value of antlers, certainly of the largest antlers, may be as advertisements. On the traditional breeding grounds of late fall, a mule buck with really heavy bone growth on its head needs only body language and posturing to impress and attract females and, at least most of the time, to intimidate other males and keep them at a distance from does in estrus.

But no matter what the value of antlers to the deer, they certainly have fascinated humans, especially hunters. Because of their great beauty, symmetry, and size (relative to body weight), the antlers of mule deer are especially valued as trophies. In many parts of the West, in fact, a hunter's standing in the community is determined by the size of the mule deer heads hanging in his or her office or living room.

Bowhunting Gold

Toward the end of August 1994, bowhunter Bruce Felker sat motionless in his tree stand in northern Arizona. A buck so huge that it seemed unreal, which he had glimpsed several days before, was now slowly approaching. Felker drew and released an arrow, which struck the animal in its left shoulder, piercing its lung and heart.

Felker still cannot believe what he found dead on the ground that day. The antlers, still in the velvet, had long drop tines on each side. The rack had twelve points on one side and sixteen on the other. Later, official scorers of both the Boone and Crockett Club and the Pope and Young Club would agree that it scored 264 6/8 points by the Boone and Crockett scoring system, a new world bow-hunting record for a nontypical mule deer.

But that is almost an understatement. When any horn or antler record is broken, which is not often, it is usually only by inches or fractions of inches. But Felker's buck measured 31 1/8 inches, or points, greater than the largest ever taped before in this category!

Top: This closeup photo illustrates how the coronet of the antlers connects to the pedicles at the top of the skull. Above: This outstanding prairie mule deer is old and probably past his prime antler growth. Though classified as a non-typical head, this is still a great trophy.

This eastern Colorado buck was able not only to breed with females, but also to drive other bucks from the vicinity, despite being badly injured in a duel or a collision with a car. It had to pursue romance on three legs.

Casting the Crown

One warm spring morning while hunting morel mushrooms on the bench of Deep Creek near my home in Montana, I flushed a porcupine from dense, green cover into a pine tree. At the base of the tree, I found a whitened, discarded antler of a mule deer, on which the porcupine had been gnawing. At other times and in other places, I've found such antlers, which other rodents, ground squirrels, chipmunks, and mice have also eaten as a good source of calcium. There are even reports of the deer themselves trying to eat cast antlers.

It is good to know that the crowning glory of a mule deer buck is never wasted, but is recycled.

The owner of these antlers was a casualty of winter, starvation, or predators. But the pure bone will be recycled by such gnawing creatures of the forest as this red squirrel.

Left: Well before sunrise, an Alberta buck follows on the lakeshore trail of a promising female. The annual rut goes on night and day.

The Terrible Lesson of the Kaibab

"We have here a very big problem. . . . Severe criticism of the Service will result unless the problem is handled with all the tact and ingenuity we are capable of putting into it."
—In a letter to the Forest Service's Chief Forester William B. Greeley written on November 24, 1922. Letter from the National Archives.

Only a hundred years ago, one of the greatest deer herds on earth still roamed in almost complete genetic isolation on the high Kaibab Plateau of northern Arizona, on the north rim of the Grand Canyon. About three thousand Rocky Mountain mule deer, outstanding and well known among trophy hunters for their great size and massive antlers, lived in harmony on this cool seven-thousand-foot-high mesa along with the many large predators that preyed on them. For Navajo and Paiute Indians, this had long been a traditional hunting ground. Every autumn for centuries they traveled here to collect winter supplies of meat and deer hides. They had little interest in heavy antlers.

The early Kaibab was also a botanist's paradise. Groves of pine, fir, and aspen grew tall among broad, grassy meadows that seemed aflame with wildflowers in summer. Later the aspens colored the forest edges a bright gold. No permanent major streams flowed through the Kaibab, which was surrounded by deep canyons (such as the Grand Canyon of the Colorado River just south) and deserts. But we will never see a place or a deer herd to match this one again, thanks to decades of incredible human bumbling and greed.

Early Game Management

Just before the turn of the century, cattle ranchers and herds of livestock were beginning to invade the Kaibab Plateau. As early as 1900, when the plateau was included in the Grand Canyon National Forest Reserve, about 220,000 cattle, sheep, and horses were already chewing and trampling the vegetation down to bare ground. By 1906, the livestock had already destroyed some of the perennial range grass cover, and for the first time ever, raw gullies appeared to mar this land where livestock did not belong at all. The deer were disappearing here as they were elsewhere in America at that time.

Unrestricted market hunting had all but eliminated buffalo, elk, moose, and pronghorns from much of the West, especially along railroads. Deer became so scarce nationwide that only a few states could still hold brief open hunting seasons. No wonder the pioneer conservationist and founder of the Boone and Crockett Club, President Theodore Roosevelt, worried about the future of wildlife in the United States. When he learned about the Kaibab, he reacted immediately and with the best intentions.

Although mule deer bucks seldom grow the massive antlers of long ago, some fairly good heads are still seen on the Kaibab.

Above: View of the Kaibab Plateau today, a vastly different environment than the botanical paradise before the invasion of cattle ranchers. Facing page: These Arizona does are alert to danger as they wade a narrow, intermittent stream.

On November 28, 1906, Roosevelt created the one-million-acre (400,000-hectare) Grand Canyon National Game Preserve as part of his new National Forest Service. He instructed the service to give every priority immediately to the "propagation and breeding of mule deer" in the new sanctuary. Unfortunately, it was no solution to the problem.

Although scientific game management was then in its infancy, and no one knew much about managing deer, Roosevelt's foresters began their task of deer restoration with enthusiasm. The first and most logical way to protect deer, it seemed to them (and to almost everyone) was to ban all hunting. This was easy to do on the Kaibab because of its remoteness and isolation. No one remembered that hunting by the Indians for countless generations had had no impact whatsoever on deer numbers.

The second "logical" step was to declare total war on predators. Coyotes, mountain lions, and bobcats abounded, and there were a few gray wolves making a last stand. Those predators had hunted Kaibab deer there even before the Indians. Navajo religion held the coyote sacred, and the Indian hunters seldom bothered to pursue the lions or wolves with which they coexisted. But with the establishment of the new game preserve, all the wild killers had to go.

Government "hunters" moved into the Kaibab with poison, traps, snares, guns, and a vengeance. During the next twenty-five years the body count was 4,889 coyotes, 781 lions, 554 bobcats, and the last 20 wolves. Uncounted others were believed killed by bounty hunters employed by cattle ranchers.

Such was the extent of the early "management" of the Kaibab deer. Apparently no one even considered the factor of livestock as a problem. Livestock grazing actually increased from 1906 to 1913, because the theory then was that livestock and deer could use the same range without competition. Cattle and sheep are grass-eaters; deer are predominately browsers and feed largely on the leaves and twigs of woody plants. It was thought that there was no conflict between the two. But of course that was not true. Besides, it was common

Above: The last gray wolves surviving in Arizona were wiped out during the predator pogrom on the Kaibab early in the 1900s. The extermination of these animals was intended to revive sagging deer numbers. Right: Early in the century, predators, rather than the proliferation of livestock that consumed the land, were erroneously blamed for the decline of deer on the Kaibab. As a result, professional hunters virtually eliminated the cougar.

knowledge that even more cattle than those allowed by permits were devouring the plateau's flora. Half-wild range stock from the surrounding desert was attracted to the plateau by its greener forage, and in addition, many of the "legal" stockmen exceeded their animal quotas. There was almost no way to monitor them.

More Problems, More Management

For the first few years, the Kaibab experiment seemed a magnificent success. Without predators, deer numbers increased each season. But almost unnoticed was the lack of large-antlered males. Within a decade, the herd doubled in size and, two years later, doubled again. In 1918, deer numbers were estimated at fifteen thousand, or five times the original number. Admittedly, however, there were no accurate means to census deer herds at that time.

Now new danger signals were flashing. In spite of a reduction in livestock permits to ten thousand, the range continued to deteriorate. All of the most nutritious forage grasses were gone, and cattle had to feed more heavily on woody plants, in direct competition with the deer, especially on the winter range. Gullies eroded the slopes. In 1919, E. A. Goldman, a federal mammalogist, began a study that lasted several years, and each of his annual reports expressed growing alarm. By 1922, he estimated the deer population exceeded twenty thousand head, or almost seven times what the range could support. "Unless the number is controlled," Goldman wrote in understatement, "irreparable damage to summer range and parts of the winter range can be expected." This mildly worded report was the first clear-cut call for deer population control.

By 1923, there were at least thirty thousand deer, about ten times the range carrying capacity, and the herd was still growing. Some unofficial estimates placed the number at one hundred thousand. However, let me emphasize again that this figure was not the result of an accurate census. Former congressman George Shiras III, a pioneer wildlife photographer, inspected the range and reported that "from 30,000 to 40,000 deer are on the verge of starvation." He described range conditions as "deplorable."

That prodded Secretary of Agriculture Henry C. Wallace into action. He appointed a nongovernmental Kaibab Deer Investigating Committee made up of lead-ing conservationists. The committee inspected the plateau in the late summer, and like Shiras, the members were appalled by what they found.

Originally there were about 700,000 acres (280,000 hectares) of deer range on the Kaibab, 300,000 acres (120,000 hectares) each of excellent summer and winter range and 100,000 acres (40,000 hectares) more of intermediate value. Under normal conditions, the deer spent spring and summer in forest margins of the upper slopes. In winter they moved down into the brush-filled canyons east and west of the plateau. Browsed periodically, the range has an opportunity to recover between seasons.

But overuse by both deer and cattle had altered the country to a dusty moonscape. Now so many inferior deer infested the summer range that many important plants, like the snowberry, had vanished completely. Aspens and Douglas firs, desperation forage, were stripped of foliage higher than a tall man's head. Few young trees and shrubs survived. Topsoil washed away. Scrawny deer chewed on anything that appeared above the hard, bare soil.

But the winter range was in even worse shape. Long before cold weather, swarms of deer invaded the canyons to feed on forage that was needed to carry them through the winter. Many of the cliff roses and almost inedible junipers were dead. Sagebrush was heavily damaged, and thin, hungry mule deer stood slowly starving.

The committee recommended immediate and drastic action. All livestock not owned by local residents would be removed immediately. (Actually *all* livestock should have been removed.) The deer population should be halved as quickly as possible. The panel suggested a three-phase program: Livetrap the deer and move them to new range; institute liberal, regulated sport hunting; and, if necessary, hire professional hunters to shoot the surplus animals.

Again the Forest Service acted promptly. It did again reduce grazing quotas, but should have eliminated them altogether. It built traps to catch deer, which were offered for sale at thirty-five dollars a head. But the traps caught very few mule deer, and no one was interested in buying any. There was no railroad near the Kaibab, and the thin, starving deer marked for relocation had to be carted out over some of the most rugged country left in America.

Facing page: The Kaibab is never more beautiful than in autumn when quaking aspens color the high plateau with gold.

Paradise Lost

Before the arrival of Anglos and their cattle around 1700, the Kaibab Plateau was a rich, green ecosystem, one which we will never really know. Nothing like this land, isolated from its surroundings for millions of years, where ponderosa pines towered over everything, and where as much as twenty feet of snow could fall in winter, exists unaltered anywhere on earth today. We know that meadows running through the forests were lush with wildflowers in summer. But which wildflowers? The "original" Kaibab was gone before its plant life could be accurately identified or inventoried.

Besides the magnificent mule deer herd, we know that wolves and cougars were fairly numerous. These predators kept the deer numbers low enough to spare impact on the environment. At the same time, predator numbers were regulated by their food supply, namely the deer and smaller creatures. It's called the balance of nature.

A number of endemic subspecies also evolved as a result of the Kaibab's long isolation. One of these, the Kaibab squirrel, survives in modest numbers. It is similar and related to the tassel-eared or Abert's squirrel, which lives on the Grand Canyon's South Rim, but the two are noticeably different. Interdependent with the ponderosa pine forests in which it lives, the Kaibab squirrel was probably much more abundant and easily seen a century ago than it is today.

In late September and early October, the aspens seem to be aflame on the land beyond the Grand Canyon's North Rim, a paradise that was nearly lost.

When trapping failed, the Forest Service asked Arizona to open a special hunting season on the Kaibab. Governor George Hunt personally inspected the range, and in late 1924, for the first time in nearly twenty years, it again became legal to shoot deer on the Kaibab. The terms of the hunt today might seem a bargain: For five dollars anyone could take three deer of either sex. But the offer came too late in the season. The one-hundred-mile (160 km) trip from Flagstaff, Arizona, over a terrible road, across the unbridged Colorado River, and up steep grades, discouraged almost all. A few hunters killed 675 deer, about one-tenth the number that had been born that spring.

A Last Resort

As a last resort, the Forest Service decided on more direct action: Surplus deer would be killed by government hunters. But Zane Grey, the popular Ohio outdoorsman and novelist, had another idea. Why not use unemployed cowboys, Grey argued, to drive the deer off the Kaibab Plateau onto better range? That way the killing would be unnecessary. Harebrained as the scheme was, a local cattle rancher, George McCormick,

was contracted to drive "not less than 3,000 nor more than 8,000 deer" southward across the Colorado River.

The great Kaibab deer drive was the worst, but perhaps the best-publicized, fiasco in wildlife management history. McCormick hired 125 cowboys and Navajos to do the herding. On a cold winter morning, his "cavalry" deployed in a great crescent that half-surrounded a small part of the winter range. At a signal, all advanced. Deer flushed before them, and soon hundreds of muleys bounded ahead of the advancing cowboys and Indians. The excited riders closed in at a gallop, whooping and beating brush with coiled lariats, Hollywood style. Success seemed within reach.

But of course it didn't work. Many deer checked their flight and dodged right back through eroded canyons. Other animals broke through thickets that horsemen couldn't negotiate and escaped. Not one deer was moved. Not one.

Now paid hunters were the only alternative. But American sportsmen opposed this inevitable "waste" of the deer. What's more, publicists in Arizona had been touting the Kaibab herd as "the biggest in the world," and a potential tourist attraction. For them,

Facing page: This young buck, here with a grazing doe, has survived the Arizona hunting season. Trophy hunters likely would have passed up this small rack. Overleaf: A late-autumn sun falls on a mule deer buck near the North Rim of the Grand Canyon, Arizona.

there could *never* be too many deer. The state game department also objected bitterly on jurisdictional grounds. The outcry of these forces was swelled by the first of the animal rights activists who opposed even the thought of "cold-blooded shooting." Few if any of the latter had ever seen how nature deals with surplus deer, by slow starvation.

Probably the biggest stumbling block to herd control turned out to be, as usual, a politician, Arizona's governor. Although Governor Hunt recognized the need for some control, he bitterly opposed "regulation" by any federal agency. He hated all of them. Henceforth, he announced, the Kaibab was to be treated as any other deer range in Arizona, one buck per hunter per season. All local hunters could hold free statewide licenses; non-residents paid twenty dollars each. Hunt threatened to call out the National Guard to enforce the game law if federal foresters killed any of "his" deer, and he secured an injunction to block any killing except by licensed hunters. Over the next four years, hunter kill averaged fewer than seven hundred, and those were mostly small bucks. It was a drop in the proverbial bucket.

Left: A wary buck skulks in the mottled sunlight of late afternoon on Arizona's Kaibab Plateau. Above: A young mule deer buck looks up from grazing.

What is Wildlife Management?

Wildlife or game management is the process of raising and then maintaining populations of game animals at high, if not the highest, level. This is done by restricting human use of the land, by planting and reforestation, by restricting the harvest (hunting) of game animals, by restocking, or by any combination of these. In modern times there have been both successes and failures. The restoration of pronghorn antelope and wild turkeys to some abundance after both had almost disappeared from the American scene are certainly among the successes.

Since World War II, a whole new profession of game managers, or game technicians or biologists, has become important. Today as many as 200,000 game

Wild turkeys share the Kaibab with mule deer and are most easily seen during the spring strutting season.

or wildlife managers may be employed by the federal governments of the United States and Canada, by the states and provinces, as well as on many private lands. More and more they depend on the latest scientific tools to do a better job of wildlife management.

Recently, many wildlife conservationists and environmentalists have been insisting that even the newest, most modern game management is not always in our best interests. They believe that we should be managing—saving and improving—entire ecosystems rather than individual species. Since much of the money to finance wildlife management has come from the sales of hunting licenses and permits, most of the funds have been spent on the major game species.

Meanwhile, deer by the thousands starved and froze to death every winter. But each spring, the losses were more than replaced by new fawns, also destined to starve. For practical purposes the Kaibab had now become a desert, populated with gaunt, parasite-ridden animals that were caricatures of the once handsome and sleek Kaibab mule deer.

A New Approach to Management Begins

The first break in this grim gridlock came in 1928. The U.S. Supreme Court ruled that the federal foresters had both a right and an obligation to protect the range in their charge. That winter, government hunters shot nearly twelve hundred deer. A few months later, Arizona's legislature created the Arizona Game and Fish Commission to take the fate of the deer away from politicians. Thus began a long overdue era of state-federal cooperation in efforts to cure the massive ills of the Kaibab.

One of the first acts of the new commission was to declare special deer hunting seasons. During the fall of 1929, nearly thirty-five hundred hunters took four thousand deer; in 1930 the legal kill rose to about five thousand. The Forest Service, on its part, began fencing the entire plateau to keep out stray cattle. It tightened control over livestock operators, and it built and improved hunter access roads. The killing of predators stopped.

By 1931, starvation, disease, malnutrition, and the shooting had reduced the deer to fewer than twenty thousand. That was still excessive, but it relieved some of the intolerable pressures of the recent past. The range began to recover. Slightly. New grasses and herbs grew on some denuded slopes; in the canyons the cliff roses, junipers, and sage appeared for the first time in years. And with improvement of the range, the deer, too, began to recover both in health and reproductive vigor.

By 1945, conditions seemed so favorable that Arizona reinstated the buck-only law for hunting. Deer numbers again may have approached a rough estimate of thirty-seven thousand. Again, there was no accurate census available, but browse lines once more began to climb the trees in the uplands, signaling a scarcity of desirable browse. Conditions were aggravated by drought, and the vital plants on the winter range added

This northern Arizona buck is in single-minded pursuit of a doe that is surely coming into estrus.

The growth, general health, and longevity of mule deer depend on the quality of their range. When overgrazing by livestock leaves the ground bare, the outlook for all wildlife is bleak. When the range is healthy, so are the deer.

very little growth. Most of the does, fawns, and yearlings entered the winter in poor condition. In spite of a record hunter kill that autumn, winter brought a major dieoff; in 1955 the prehunt deer population plummeted to an estimated twelve thousand, the lowest since about 1916, but still four times the Kaibab's true capacity.

Two Lessons from the Kaibab

Since then, management of the Kaibab mule deer has been based more on scientific principles than on guesswork, emotion, and politics. The herd and the land are nothing like they were before cattle ranchers, livestock, and predator controllers appeared on that unique high plateau. A good many mule deer live there now, but the body size and antlers of bucks are small compared to those magnificent specimens of the past. Decades of blundering and greed have squandered a matchless wildlife resource there beyond the north rim of the Grand Canyon.

But two lessons can be learned from this debacle. The first: Inviolate refuges for grazing and browsing animals such as deer will become death traps when predators, human hunters, or both are removed. The predators' natural role is to keep plant-eaters in balance with their food supply. When the balance is upset, humans must function as the controlling agent if they want vigorous wildlife living on a healthy range.

The second lesson: Neither mule deer nor any of the other ungulates can survive long where the range is degraded year after year by too many sheep and cattle. Already too much livestock has ruined too much land in the American West—and the world—and that process is ongoing, as I will illustrate later. Most of our professional wildlife managers, as well as our hunting and nonhunting public, have learned those lessons, but too many range managers and most politicians have not. Perhaps their eyes and minds are closed. There is so much to be learned from the terrible lesson of the Kaibab, but only time will tell if we have paid any attention.

Mule Deer Country

"O, give me a home where the buffalo roam,
Where the deer and the antelope play,
Where seldom is heard a discouraging word,
And the skies are not cloudy all day."
—From "Home on the Range," Brewster Higley, 1873

Earlier in life, when my legs and lungs were more willing, and a lot stronger, I probably spent too much time exploring and backpacking in the colorful canyonlands of the American Southwest. One of my favorite "discoveries" was the West Rim Trail in Utah's Zion National Park. As spectacular as it was steep, the trail began with a nearly vertical climb through misnamed Refrigerator Canyon to pause at Scout Lookout, followed by an even steeper pull past a series of switchbacks called Walters Wiggles. In springtime, wildflowers grew wherever they could gain a roothold, even from cracks in the canyon walls. If I started before daybreak, as I usually did to beat the intense heat later on, canyon wrens would be singing and my water supply would last longer. By noon I would reach a different, more level landscape, but one still surrounded by red rock monoliths. This was the true backcountry of Zion that too few ever see. In those days, I had it all to myself.

Zion was and still is a region rich with wildlife. Always I found mule deer, turkeys, and once, a black bear. On my first morning camping in that fragrant, dry wilderness, I was awakened by noises just outside my tent. Unzipping the flaps, I stared directly into two beautiful faces damp with morning dew. A doe and her fawn were clearly puzzled at the strange orange Gore-Tex shelter and were sniffing it. But the unshaven face in the zippered entrance was more than the mother could handle. She bounded away a short distance, stopped, and stared back again in total disbelief.

No matter what time of the year I spent vagabonding in Zion Park, I would meet mule deer, usually herds of them. It was here that I first realized that much of the dry southwestern United States is excellent mule deer country. I spotted them occasionally in the Coalpits Wash section of the park where only a few inches of rain fall every year. I also found them at about seven thousand feet (2,130 m) elevation on the high plateaus, which receive about two feet (0.6 m) of rain annually. But year in and year out, the muleys were most easily observed in fall in Zion Canyon, through which flows the Virgin River. Vegetation along the banks of the river is thicker and more varied than elsewhere in the park and the deer depend heavily on this forage. But the deer in the valley must also cope with great extremes in temperature, where in six months' time it may vary from 115 degrees Fahrenheit (46 degrees Celsius) in July to -15 degrees Fahrenheit (-26 degrees Celsius) in January.

Flowage from Emerald Pool in Zion National Park, Utah.

Bryce Canyon National Park in southern Utah has many mule deer. But the spectacular scenery of the park rivals the beautiful wildlife.

Among the finest mule deer I have ever seen was a dark-gray, fat buck that spent one November evening splashing back and forth across the Virgin, trying to follow two does on opposite banks at once. While sitting down to change film in my camera, I saw the reason for his nervous behavior. Another buck, which may have rivaled the splasher in antler size, was following the action from a distance and seemed ready to move in. Darkness came before I learned how this chapter in the mating season ended.

If the mule deer population of Zion maintains a balance, within the carrying capacity of its stark range, this can be attributed to a good population of mountain lions or cougars, which keep the deer from growing too numerous and degrading the quality of the range. In addition, some wander outside the park and are shot during legal open seasons. Although, I have never seen a cougar here, I have often found footprints and scat, especially in the Kolob Canyon sector. Also, the caterwauling I heard one night while camped near Kolob could only have come from a lovesick cat.

Bryce Canyon National Park, Utah

Bryce Canyon, a short drive from Zion, is another of those southwestern, desert national parks where it is too easy to miss the mule deer and other wild creatures, while savoring the stupendous canyon scenery. Bryce Canyon really isn't a canyon, but the eroded edge of the high Paunsaugunt Plateau. It is a vast area of salmon- and red-toned hoodoos—strange, earthen shapes formed by wind and water erosion, whose hues become less and then more intense as the sun migrates from east to west. If you can resist driving from overlook to scenic overlook, and instead hike the many rim trails, you will meet coyotes and nuthatches, Steller's jays and Clark's nutcrackers, badgers and blue grouse (the male displaying in courtship if it is April), chipmunks and gray foxes, golden-mantled ground squirrels and endangered Utah prairie dogs, all sharing this country with the mule deer. If you are lucky, are a keen wildlife spotter, or best of all, both, you just might meet a bobcat as we did near a busy trailhead parking lot.

Above and left: Gray foxes and bobcats thrive in Bryce Canyon. Both can be seen at times by alert hikers on well-maintained trails.

Facing page: This mule buck is sleek and fat in the fall, after a summer spent in the undisturbed wilderness backcountry.
Above: Three mule deer bucks on the grasslands of the central United States. This part of the country is in great contrast to the Rockies, but muleys thrive where the land is not overgrazed by livestock.

The mule deer of Bryce move among three life zones with the seasons and with the availability of browse, as they do elsewhere on deserts. At the bottom of the canyon and below seven thousand feet (2,130 m) is the juniper-piñon zone where precipitation averages about a foot (30 cm) per year. But it is enough to sustain the juniper trees, Gambel oaks, and piñon pines, all providing deer and their allies with food in autumn. Deer concentrate here especially during years when acorns and pine nut crops are good.

At about eight thousand feet (2,440 m) above sea level, green-leaf manzanita is an abundant plant, in some places growing as the understory beneath tall ponderosa pines. The spruce-fir-aspen zone is the highest, lying at about nine thousand feet, and is best known for the bristlecone pines, one of which may be seventeen hundred years old. In springtime, wildflowers carpet some of this upper zone, and the deer and their compatriots eat many of them.

The Great Plains

The Great Plains of North America were created from sediment washed and blown eastward out of the Rocky Mountains for millions of years. For about eight hundred miles (1,300 km) the plains gradually slope downward from the base of the Rockies to the Mississippi River. Specifically, three fairly distinct zones of prairie evolved. Closest to the Rockies and adjacent to the range's rain shadow is the strip or belt (extending north to south) of shortgrass prairie. With the least rainfall, the blue gramma and buffalo grasses here rarely grow higher than twelve inches (30 cm).

The belt farthest east and paralleling the Mississippi has the heaviest rainfall, about thirty inches (76 cm) annually, and thus is the tallgrass prairie. When our pioneer ancestors drove covered wagons westward through this prairie, they sometimes found big bluestem and other native grasses growing higher than a man sitting on his horse. Between the short- and

Prairie Dogs and Mule Deer

All of the creatures of the plains depend on one another, at least to some extent, as do the animals in any ecosystem. Early one South Dakota spring near Wind Cave National Park, I noticed that a small band of mule deer never wandered far from a black-tailed prairie dog town. Detested by ranchers, prairie dogs live in densely packed, often very extensive colonies where by midsummer they have eaten most of the vegetation down to the bare ground. It doesn't seem that any wild animals could live long on this bare earth. There is no better place, however, to see everything from rattlesnakes and badgers to golden eagles, burrowing owls, and red-tailed and ferruginous hawks, either hunting or using the prairie dog burrows for shelter. A century ago, most dog towns also had their resident black-footed ferrets, which by 1987 had been exterminated. (Ferrets are now being reintroduced in Wyoming with some success.) Over 130 different species of vertebrates have some reason to visit or even live in prairie dog colonies at some time. But mule deer?

I didn't watch too long before I discovered at least one reason they were nearby. Here around the perimeter of the town, the first nutritious green shoots of

Few of the once extensive prairie dog towns of the Great Plains remain. But here and there in sanctuaries the busy rodents are very important to other grassland wildlife.

the season were appearing, before they grew anywhere else, and the muleys were taking full advantage of it. What happens here is that the prairie dogs aerate the soil by their digging and then fertilize it with their droppings. Then by clipping the vegetation very short, their unique visual early-warning system for predators, they also keep the fresh green plants at a nutritious stage longer than in the surrounding area. Antelope as well as the deer benefit.

tallgrass zones was a mixed grass prairie of midsized grasses unique to that area. Altogether these three bands of prairie once comprised the largest and finest grassland in the world. It stretched uninterrupted over a fourth of the contiguous United States and included a vast area of southern Canada.

We know this matchless wilderness supported about sixty million bison and maybe an equal number of pronghorns. It was the home of mule deer, elk, Audubon's bighorn sheep, plains grizzly bears, and plains (or buffalo) wolves. The number of prairie dogs was astronomical, numbering perhaps five billion. Probably half the waterfowl on the continent were born beside prairie potholes. Today the bears, sheep, and wolves are gone. So are the bison and elk, except for scattered small bands in small parks. Probably more plant species than we realize have disappeared. The prairie is still an important duck nesting area, but only a fraction as many nest as did two centuries ago. Of all the large mammals only the pronghorns and mule

deer have survived in significant numbers. Some areas of the Great Plains still remain important mule deer country.

The best places to find plains muleys now are on public lands, particularly the national parks, in the shortgrass zone: Wind Cave and Badlands National Parks and Custer State Park in South Dakota, Theodore Roosevelt National Park in North Dakota, and Devil's Tower National Monument in Wyoming. Some of the other wildlife you still surely see are the birds of prey (prairie falcons, golden eagles, red-tailed, Swainson's and ferruginous hawks, burrowing and shorteared owls), such mammal meat-eaters as coyotes, red and swift foxes, and badgers, and a varying cast of creatures from dung beetles, many species of mice and gophers, and rattlesnakes to meadow larks, killdeers, and goldfinches. Even today, consumed by ranching and agriculture, fencing, and other human development, the Great Plains support a surprising amount of wildlife. That includes, of course, thousands of mule deer.

Facing page, top: Keeping one eye on the photographer, this fine muley buck stays close to a doe grazing on an adjacent slope. Facing page, bottom: Bighorn sheep (this ram photographed in Alberta) once lived in badlands areas of the Great Plains. Today all are gone.

Above: Black bears, like this one clawing a tree to mark his territory, range thoughout the North American west. But luckily for their muley neighbors, black bears are partial to a supper of insects and only rarely will kill a healthy mule deer. Left: This alert Alberta doe is constantly using all of her keen senses of sight, smell, and hearing to monitor what happens around her.

The Rocky Mountains

For a long time my favorite mule deer country has been in the Rocky Mountains. In this great range, or series of ranges, stretching from Mexico northward almost to the Yukon, one special place to find and watch mule deer year-round is always Grand Teton National Park. This 310,500-acre (124,200-hectare) sanctuary in northwestern Wyoming is best known for the spectacular mountain uplift that ranks very high among the most dramatic and beautiful mountain landscapes on earth. But for me the park is much more than that. From about sixty-five hundred feet (183 m) into the Snake River Valley and Jackson Hole, to the summit of Grand Teton, the park's highest peak, at almost fourteen thousand feet (4,265 m), are uncut evergreen and aspen forests, sagebrush flats, canyons, and alpine lakes. All of these habitats and life zones are accessible by a fine trail system that makes it easy and most pleasant to hike through the finest of mule deer country. Jackson Hole was also our home for nearly twenty years.

Compared to the mule deer country on the Great Plains and in the southwestern deserts, spring comes late in the Tetons. During some winters as much as fifteen feet of snow will have fallen in the highest elevations, and it isn't until the end of April that the first wildflowers, sage buttercups, begin to bloom. But two to three months later, the eastern slopes of the Tetons offer the greatest wildflower show in the world. The summer mountainsides and high meadows riot with bright colors.

Mule deer share this paradise with elk and Shiras moose, with ground squirrels, marmots, and chipmunks, with mountain bluebirds, thrushes, warblers, great gray owls, golden eagles, and more than two hundred other species of birds. Peggy and I have hiked for thousands of miles on Teton Trails and except for once being trapped all day long in a light mountain tent during a cold sudden rain, there were no dull or unpleasant times. The number of mule deer—including our largest ever—we met per mile of trail probably averaged higher than anywhere else. It was an excellent park in which to study the Rocky Mountain subspecies of muley at all seasons.

Just spotting or (better still) photographing a mule buck such as this one is excuse enough to spend fall days out in western mule deer range.

104

Facing page: An autumn scene northwest of Apgar Village in Glacier National Park, Montana. Both mule and whitetailed deer live in this area. Above: A mule deer buck of the northern Rockies searches in the moonlight for females in estrus.

The deer spend winters in the river bottoms, along the Snake and Gros Ventre Rivers and Flat Creek, sometimes venturing out of Grand Teton Park into the town of Jackson, into gardens and local golf courses. Along with moose, they browse the willows growing around beaver ponds. One doe would occasionally sleep beneath the back deck of our house overlooking the Snake River valley. I think that later her twin fawns were born just beyond our bedroom window one morning in June.

As summer progresses, most of the mule deer gradually migrate upward, always staying well below the retreating snow line. In August, hikers can see them, especially the bachelor males still in velvet, when backpacking along the Teton Crest Trail and dipping down into Alaska Basin on the Idaho side of the Teton Range. Up here the deer live with black bears, pikas, Uinta ground squirrels, Clark's nutcrackers, and gray-capped rosy finches. This Teton high country is free of cattle and therefore has a pristine look much different from in the adjacent Targhee National Forest where too

many mountain slopes and meadows have a degraded look from the overgrazing of livestock.

One of our Teton memories was a very sad one. On a clear day late in winter, to cope with a bad case of cabin fever, Peggy and I hiked the trail that leads to Bradley and Taggart Lakes. In summertime the human traffic on these trails is heavy, but this January day we found only the tracks of a coyote and of several mule deer. When we reached an overlook above white, frozen Taggart Lake, we looked down toward where the deer tracks led. Immediately we saw five deer following a game trail around the lake. But one of the animals turned to walk directly across the lake, apparently taking a shortcut. Near the middle, the deer stopped as the ice began to crack all around it. A hole opened up, and the deer slid into the frigid water.

We watched for a long while, but could see no way that it was remotely possible to save the animal. It swam in circles, now and then putting both front feet on the ice at the edge of the watery hole, but the ice was too thin to support it and would break off, another

107

Facing page: A mule deer buck in Glacier National Park, Montana. Above: Cow parsnip, a common browse of mule deer, grows against the mountainous backdrop of Glacier National Park.

bobbing slab in the dark water. Although obviously weakening, the deer attempted again and again to gain solid footing, and each time failed. The deer's companions continued to walk, never looking back. We tried not to look back, either.

Palo Duro Canyon State Park, Texas

Perhaps the most dramatic of all mule deer country survives in an isolated, little-known section of the north Texas Panhandle. Palo Duro Canyon is a deep gash carved out of the flat, dry Texas high plain by the Prairie Dog Fork of the Red River. The canyon is about 120 miles (192 km) long, 20 miles (32 km) wide, and 800 feet (244 m) deep. Part of the canyon is Palo Duro State Park, arguably the finest state park in America.

Discovering Palo Duro from high on the treeless rim for the first time fascinates and disquiets. The steep canyon walls embody a haunting beauty in red, purple-gray, and brown hues. The multicolored layers of soil have eroded into strange formations called Spanish skirts, named for their resemblance to the flaring dresses of Latin dancers. Through most of the nineteenth century, Palo Duro was Comanche country, and native wildlife must have been plentiful.

The names of the native plants are almost as colorful as the canyon: skunkbush sumac (a favorite of deer), shinoak, mountain mahogany, trailing ratany, bladderpod, halfshrub sundrop, globemallow.

But trouble reached paradise when Captain Charles Goodnight, who would become legendary for "taming" this little-known region, arrived to establish the first cattle ranch along Prairie Dog Fork more than a century ago. In the process, Goodnight, and his hard-riding crew, drove an estimated ten thousand buffalo, and along with them most of the mule deer, out of the canyon.

Muleys were still fairly rare in the 1950s when the Texas Department of Parks and Wildlife restocked the canyon with several hundred desert mule deer live-trapped in the Trans-Pecos region farther west. At the time, state wildlife researchers noticed that wild turkeys were fairly abundant and that whitetailed deer also were present. Nobody knows exactly how or when the whitetails had moved into the canyon. Some old timers insist that a few were there all along. The whitetails seemed to be getting along with the mule deer.

Maybe a mistake was made later in the 1950s when aoudads, or Barbary sheep, were released in the canyon. Releasing any nonnative species into an ecosystem always carries great risk of displacing native species and damaging the environment. Natives of the Atlas Mountains of North Africa, where they are endangered today, aoudads are neither sheep nor goats, but in habits and appearance they resemble both. They prefer steep, rugged country, and their rich, red coats blend well into Palo Duro's canyon walls. Not surprisingly the aoudads have prospered and like the mule deer are now hunted outside the state park boundaries.

Drive down into Palo Duro Park today just before dawn, and you will soon meet many of the wild residents. Roadrunners race across the narrow winding road. From a discreet distance, coyotes watch you pass. Turkeys are easily seen. At higher elevations and especially along the rim stand herds of mule deer. Some of the bucks carry the best antlers for the species in all Texas. Down toward the canyon bottom, particularly around the campgrounds and beside permanent water pools of Prairie Dog Fork, are most of the whitetails. But during several camping-photography trips, we have had only brief looks at the aoudads, which are much warier than the mule deer. Nonetheless they are there in substantial numbers. They may even be increasing to the detriment of the deer. Biologists and some ranchers living in the area have noticed that mule deer tend to leave areas occupied by grazing aoudads.

There also may be a problem with the whitetails. There is increasing evidence that whitetailed and mule deer are crossbreeding. Researcher Suzy Stubblefield found that about 6 percent of bucks taken by hunters in the canyon outside of the park were hybrids. On one ranch, one in four bucks harvested was a hybrid. It is a cause of concern because native mule deer could eventually be bred out of existence here. Most of the crosses seem to come from mule deer bucks and whitetail does.

The Prairie Dog Fork meanders through Palo Duro Canyon State Park, Texas, the home of both mule and whitetailed deer.

Above: Hybrids, or crosses between mule deer and whitetails, are common in Palo Duro Canyon State Park, Texas. Facing page: An introduced alien, the aoudad or barbary sheep from Africa, may be furnishing too much competition for the mule deer.

Whitetailed deer with large, muley ears and mule deer with forked, whitetail antlers are not, all by themselves, evidence of crossbreeding. According to biologist Rodney Marburger, positive proof comes only from examining the metatarsal glands. Whitetails have metatarsals one inch (2.5 cm) long and creased in the middle. Mule deer metatarsals are four to five inches (10–13cm) long with no crease. As might be suspected, hybrids have two-inch (5 cm) glands with only a slight crease.

The Palo Duro crossbreeding is only one example of the way whitetails may be expanding inexorably into traditional mule deer range elsewhere, sometimes taking it over. Gradually whitetails have worked their way westward, far up such great rivers as the Yellowstone and Missouri. Where we live, in lower Paradise Valley, Montana, along the Yellowstone, whitetails are now the predominant species, especially in the bottomlands. This may be a result of behavioral peculiarities difficult to detect or from radical change in the habitat, or both. Or perhaps shyer, wiser whitetails are better able to cope with open hunting seasons.

So Palo Duro Canyon State Park is unique, as well as very important, in that it might tell us something about the mule deer's future everywhere.

The Future of Mule Deer

*"For the fate of the sons of man and the fate of the beasts is the same;
as one dies so dies the other. They all have the same breath, and man has no
advantage over the beasts; for all is vanity."*
—From Ecclesiastes, Chapter 3:19–22

Scientists generally agree that forty different species and numerous subspecies of deer inhabit the earth. Together they comprise the family Cervidae. Five of the forty species are native to North America: the moose, elk, caribou, whitetailed deer, and mule deer. Compared to deer elsewhere, all of these are at least locally abundant and are doing fairly well. But in the case of mule deer, there is no room for complacency, as we shall see.

It is interesting to note that the mule deer's range overlaps with those of all the other native deer. No doubt the species at times compete with one another. Different authorities estimated the continental mule deer population at less than four to five million animals in 1994, and that seems like an abundance. But early American writer and naturalist Ernest Thompson Seton believed there were ten million mule deer when the first Europeans in North America began to settle the land four hundred years ago. (Some modern biologists believe this estimate was much too high.) Since then there have been severe ups and downs, but during the past century or so there has been a noticeable and steady population decline.

The worst times for mule deer occurred during the early 1800s. The animals were slaughtered without regard for size, season, or increasing scarcity, to feed the men in logging camps and gold boom towns of the West, as well as the large crews then building intercontinental railroads. "Life is no joy on this frontier," one Colorado miner wrote to his family in Philadelphia, "but we have vennison [*sic*] three times every day." Completion of the railroads allowed the shipment of mule deer and other wild game to city markets far away. For a while, deer meat was cheaper than beef from Kansas City to Chicago, selling for from two to three cents a pound.

Seton estimated mule deer numbers during the early 1900s had fallen to 500,000. That was the low point. It came at a time when the first faint signs of a conservation conscience were stirring in the United States. Hunters especially were worried about the decline. As a result, unrestricted hunting ended and America's mule deer began a strong comeback.

The quality of the environment is the most important factor in the number of mule deer that survive each year. Proper management of the land—both public and private—is this month-old fawn's best chance for a secure future.

Strange as it may seem, the rutting season can be an ordeal for active mule bucks, such as this one, panting from pursuing a doe out of sight.

Managing Hunting on Behalf of the Deer

In 1960, game biologists were convinced that the mule deer population had recovered to over seven million animals. Hunting mule deer in their range was never better. Perhaps it was *too* good for the best interests of the species. The business of outfitting hunters thrived. During just one decade beginning in 1965, over six million deer were shot legally, and that was likely far too many. Game managers had overestimated how many animals could be harvested. Hunting seasons had to be cut back sharply, and in 1975, some areas were closed altogether. For example, hunters in Nevada had bagged thirty-four thousand mule deer in 1965, which was enough to temporarily halt hunting there. Since then biologists have done a much better job of managing the mule deer herds. With modern game management methods, they now have much more accurate census information available on which to base hunting seasons. For another thing—another very important thing—they have recognized the need to manage small or regional groups of mule deer within the state's overall population.

Game managers in state game and fish departments have become increasingly aware that each game species, including the mule deer, cannot be managed properly with a single strategy for the entire state. The deer in different places, now called management areas, live in unique habitats. For example, severe winters may have a more devastating effect on the animals in one part of a state than in another. Adequate rainfall would be more essential in one area than another. And reproductive success would vary with local predation. Better deer managers now take all of these factors into consideration when they plan future hunting seasons and bag limits, area by area.

Managing the Land for All of Us

Probably the best we can hope is for mule deer to maintain their present populations into the future, and that will not be easy. We know that regulation of hunting alone will not do it. There is the ugly example of the overgrazing of Arizona's Kaibab Plateau, described earlier, when all hunting was stopped and predators eliminated. What *really* determines how many mule

Above: Deepening snow drives mule deer from high summer range to traditional winter ranges at lower altitudes. This buck is on the way down. Left: This three-and-a-half-year-old buck is poised to become an outstanding trophy animal. Overleaf: Some winters, mule deer must travel long distances over open terrain for food; this makes them vulnerable to predators and poachers.

deer will roam the West is how well we manage the western lands, both public and private, which are the habitat of these animals. To date we have done a terrible job of it. Now as we come to the end of the twentieth century, some public lands are in such deplorable state that it does not bode well for any of the wild creatures that depend on them to survive, let alone prosper.

Northwest of Salt Lake City, Utah, the Wasatch Mountains rise high over the eastern rim of America's Great Basin. This was and is excellent mule deer country. Within the Wasatch is a small, twenty-five-square-mile (65-sq.-km) Eden called Red Butte Canyon that has been fenced and closed to public use since 1909. No trees were ever cut here. No livestock have ever entered the sanctuary. In contrast to the surrounding country, the canyon is a paradise of natural, native vegetation, dense and almost impenetrable especially along the deep, cool stream that flows through it.

Just to walk through Red Butte Canyon makes people realize that they have never really seen the American West as it existed before we "won" it. All at once you realize what the entire Rocky Mountain region must have looked like before it was trampled and overgrazed to what in too many places is gradually turning into semidesert. How has this happened? And why?

To begin, the various federal government agencies entrusted with the land, specifically the U.S. Forest Service, the bureaus of Land Management and Reclamation, and even the Fish and Wildlife Service, have done a poor job. But while saying that, we must also point guilty fingers at ourselves and especially at the quality of the politicians we elect to office. The men and women we send to the U.S. Senate and House of Representatives term after term after term have been like the proverbial foxes sent to guard the henhouses. Or worse. For just one example, they have permitted livestock grazing, often by far too many animals, for almost insignificant grazing fees. The cost to cattle and sheep ranchers is far less than they would pay for nongovernment land, and doubtless less than the ranchers themselves would charge if the land were theirs. This continues even today on 270 million acres (96 million hectares) of the public's property. There are two rays of hope here. First, Secretary of the Interior Bruce Babbitt, having failed to raise grazing fees in 1992 and 1993, vows he will try again in the future.

Second, there was a recent court case in which a Department of the Interior administrative law judge, John Rampton, Jr., halted further grazing in one Utah allotment until it is determined whether the environmental impact of such grazing is in the public interest. This is the first time such effects have been considered. May it be the first of many.

From the time much of the West was settled, ranchers formed a favored-status partnership with the federal government, which still owns much of the land that their cattle and sheep roam. The alliance is just as strong today, partly through old tradition, formalized by the federal Taylor Grazing Act passed in 1934, and partly thanks to western senators who owe allegiance to rancher supporters. Land-use decisions are made in the favor of livestock raisers at the expense of all other citizens. Thanks to these legislators, taxpayers—you and I—spend fifty million dollars annually to subsidize the systematic degradation of our own property.

Except in scattered national parks and a few state reserves, almost no truly pristine areas remain in the United States or Canada. For a long time, no one has kept track of the damage done by too many cattle and sheep. Not only have they destroyed important riparian areas, but they have changed the entire composition of native western flora. Today we have no idea whatever which kinds of native plants once grew in what areas. Every year or so, an inquisitive botanist finds a "new" plant growing in a tiny cemetery plot somewhere that has been protected for generations from livestock hooves and jaws, only to discover that the "new" plant was once common when only bison, pronghorns, and mule deer roamed the land. Maybe it's fortunate that we don't greatly miss what we never knew, such as the bison herds, the passenger pigeons, the streambanks lush with green vegetation, and the hillsides blanketed with summer wildflowers. These have also all but disappeared.

Streamside habitat in the West, important mule deer range, has probably suffered most from cattle hooves. Such riparian habitat destruction is hard to document or even notice. Because it happens so slowly, so subtly, it is as hard to detect as the deepening of wrinkles on your own face over the years. But at any speed, it is serious business because biologists believe that at least 75 percent of all western wildlife, which of course includes mule deer, depends on waterways and especially on the nutritious vegetation along the

Facing page: Like this buck, all mule deer are constantly alert, their senses tuned to what is happening around them.

Logging and Losses

Today American taxpayers support an overharvest of timber in national forests, which leaves the public with vast, eroding stump wastelands that make clear-cut Amazon rainforests seem like conservation areas. Hardly believable, but true, is the fact that all this lumbering has for many years meant a net monetary loss for the U. S. Forest Service. An encouraging note is that President Bill Clinton announced early in 1994 his intention to eliminate below-cost timber sales by 1998.

And if you picture the coastal forests of British Columbia as evergreen sanctuaries for wildlife, with fish jumping in pristine streams, think again. If anything, the Canadian government has permitted even more destruction of timberlands than our own authorities. Forget about finding any mule deer in such places, either in Canada or the United States.

A buck enjoying one of the last pleasant days of fall sunshine before the onset of winter, which can be brutal in mule deer country.

Nabbing Poachers

Fortunately, modern science is making it somewhat easier to apprehend poachers. Now it is easy to positively match the hair and blood of an individual deer with the dried, brown blood spots and fur found in a pickup truck, on the berm of a backroad, or on a poacher's pants. Game wardens now have the means for more immediate response to reports of illegal activities. They also have a few tricks up their sleeves.

It is illegal, of course, to shoot deer from a road. And hunters in Wyoming, for example, who spot a trophy mule deer standing tantalizingly within rifle range of a rural road, would be wise to take a long, hard look at the animal. It may be made of Styrofoam. And game wardens just may be lurking nearby. Big game animal decoys are increasingly being used to nab illegal hunters in many states because this method puts poachers and wardens in the same place at the same time.

Everywhere, poachers kill too many mule deer, often by jacklighting at night. All of us must report these crimes.

This is how it works. Say that complaints point to deer poachers working every weekend in a certain, fairly remote area. The wardens know the poachers are looking for trophy antlers to sell, because only bucks have been shot and the headless carcasses left to rot. Somewhere in this area, where no one lives within rifle range and where nothing stands in the line of fire, a warden team of three or four places a decoy near a road where it is easily spotted in the headlamps of a pickup truck. The decoy is either a full mount of a deer or a deer hide stretched carefully over a Styrofoam body. The rack is of trophy dimensions.

From concealment all around, the wardens begin the waiting game. One is assigned to videotape what happens. The others are ready to move in and arrest anyone who shoots at the decoy. Violations may be of three kinds: shooting from a road, attempting to take game illegally, and hunting without a license. Poachers can often be booked on all three charges. Sometimes the long vigil is in vain. But on other occasions, Wyoming wardens have seen poachers pump as many as nine shots into the fake deer before realizing they have been duped. For many the embarrassment of being caught shooting a dummy is almost as painful as being convicted and fined. Although it might seem that poachers would soon be aware of this ruse, law enforcement officers in Wyoming and elsewhere have been using decoys for at least ten years with considerable, and undiminished, success.

Of course decoying won't save mule deer from all their other problems, but it helps, and at least a few agencies are trying.

Facing page: A fawn's security depends on remaining inconspicuous. This one is exposed a little too much for its own good, but soon the youngster will be physically able to follow its mother.

This muley buck with antlers in the velvet hides in the green, lush, early summer vegetation. Its antlers will continue to grow for another month or so.

Above: The velvet has just peeled—or has been rubbed—from these antlers, now stained with blood. But the blood dries quickly, and in a few hours the antlers will be brown. Left: Snow begins to fall in mule deer country. This doe will likely survive the winter because browse is available at lower elevations, where she will soon migrate.

banks that also serves as cover. Keep in mind that a single Hereford cow allowed to linger in a riparian area eats six tons (5.5 tonnes) of vegetation a year. Government-required fencing would reduce some of this consumption and damage.

Not far from where we live in south-central Montana, a typical stream hurries out of the Absaroka-Beartooth Wilderness Area, eventually to reach the Yellowstone River. Downstream from the wilderness area, a number of fairly large ranches border the river and the ranchers own the riparian rights. On one of these ranches, livestock has been fenced away from the river bank. As a result, it is a cool and pleasant stretch of river from which to flycast for trout in the shade of cottonwoods, aspens, and willows of all ages. Openings among the trees are filled with layers of shrubs where mule deer often feed and rest. As Peggy and I pulled on waders and rigged fly rods here one morning, we saw or heard singing Swainson's thrushes, robins, wood pewees, a Lazuli bunting, a warbling vireo, a willow flycatcher, and several species of warblers.

Moving downstream toward the adjoining ranch is like wandering from day into night. This one does not keep cattle and horses from completely free access to the river. As a result they have eaten and trampled everything they can reach, have exposed the bare ground, and worse, have seriously broken down the banks, allowing valuable soil to continually wash away. There are no young trees here to replace the old cottonwoods that are nearing the end of their normal life span. The only birds likely to be seen here are starlings, Brewer's blackbirds, cowbirds, and perhaps a daring robin. It is not a productive section to cast for trout. Although we have driven past this ranch many times, we have never once seen a mule deer here.

The Cost of Poaching

So which is more valuable anyway, a cow or a mule deer? Steve Smith, a law enforcement officer of the Wyoming Fish & Game Department, has one answer. Recently Smith attended the trial of a man arrested for deer poaching and fined a mere $25 by a lenient judge. "The fine is excessive," the defendant claimed. "We have more deer in this state than we need, and I only killed one without a license. It wasn't worth $25 in the first place."

That made Smith mad and started him thinking.

And calculating. By checking his department's annual report, Smith learned that hunters spend an average of $75 per hunting day and that they hunt an average of almost seven days in the fall. Thus, one poached deer is a loss of about $517 to the state's economy. That figure does not take into account the cost of a hunting license, money which is then spent for conservation purposes. Nor does it take into consideration the aesthetic value of the deer lost to citizens who do not hunt, or the value to tourists who visit Wyoming to watch wildlife.

Calculating a little further, about seventy poachers are apprehended by Wyoming conservation officers every year, which means that this poaching costs Wyoming at least $36,000. Multiply that amount by seven or eight for the other mule deer hunting states.

More figuring brings more information. In 1980, University of Wyoming statistician Clynn Phillips completed a survey of amounts spent by hunters, both resident and nonresident. Nonresident deer hunters alone spent over $12 million during that hunting season for everything from socks and ammunition to gasoline and steak dinners. Now in 1995 that figure would be about $15 million, an amount of almost inestimable importance to the Wyoming economy. These numbers would apply just as well to such other mule deer states as Colorado, Utah, Idaho, Montana, Oregon, New Mexico, and Washington, as well as the province of Alberta.

While the quality of the environment is the most important factor in the number of deer that survive each year, poaching can and does take a significant toll. That is why most of the deer hunting states in the West always welcome, in fact request, citizen help and information about poaching. Most also maintain poaching "hotlines," toll-free telephone numbers that anyone can call around the clock to report violations. Callers may remain anonymous. In some states, there are cash rewards for information that leads to arrests and convictions. Far too often in too many communities, poaching is regarded as a harmless prank and then treated as such by local judges. In addition to fostering an attitude that some laws need not be obeyed, poaching is really serious business. All of us who are interested in mule deer (or any other wildlife) are honor bound to reach for the telephone when we hear about illegal hunting.

Facing page: This buck is enjoying the early, but brief, winter sunlight, storing energy for the tougher times ahead. Overleaf: Does are likely to bear fewer fawns following the worst winters because the lingering intense cold causes them to reabsorb fetuses.

The Danger of Disease from Game Farm Animals

A mule deer shot in 1993 near a game farm in the Hardin, Montana, area was diagnosed with tuberculosis. The discovery sent shock waves through the western wildlife community because it is a deadly disease among wild animals. A number of wildlife biologists have long cautioned that once the disease establishes itself in a wild herd, there are strong possibilities it will spread uncontrolled and uncontrollable throughout the entire herd.

Montana state veterinarian Clarence Siroky believes that there is little doubt that the dead animal contracted tuberculosis from the Elk Valley game farm herd. The disease was first detected among the elk on the 3,400-acre (1,360-hectare) ranch and has been traced back to animals imported from Nebraska. In 1991, thirty-five of the Elk Valley elk tested positive to tuberculosis and were destroyed. The ranch has since been under quarantine.

The infected, dead mule deer underscores a need to control a potentially disastrous situation of native game animals by more strict regulation of game farms. But the game farm industry in Montana (and elsewhere) vigorously opposes additional regulation and has enlisted support from a group called Putting People First!, which is aligned with the Wise Use Movement, a pro-mining, -timber, and –big agriculture coalition. The danger is there, but the solution to the problem may be far off.

Above: This mule deer buck in Alberta already shows excellent antler growth by mid-summer. His velvet-coated rack shows excellent growth. Left: Deer have a much better chance to last the winter in habitat where all the forests have not been clear cut and there is shelter from the bitter winds.

Stalking Mule Deer
with a Camera

"My heart's in the Highlands, my heart is not here;
My heart's in the Highlands a-chasing the deer."
—From "My Heart's in the Highlands," Robert Burns

Stalking mule deer with a camera, most recently to illustrate this book, has given Peggy and me many of the most memorable times of our lives. This species lives in some of America's most scenic country, and mule deer themselves are interesting, attractive, and unpredictable enough to make shooting them the greatest sport. And challenge.

Except perhaps for bighorn sheep, photographing mule deer has required more walking on steep wilderness trails than has stalking any other native big game. Photographing whitetailed deer, by comparison, means calling, rattling antlers, and then just waiting quietly to attract rutting bucks into photo range. I feel that I have made more footprints per picture when searching for mule deer than for any other species of the Cervidae family.

Finding Mule Deer

We have found mule deer in many unexpected places. One winter when the weather was especially dreary in Montana, we drove southward toward the Texas Big Bend country to thaw out. En route we paused for a few days of hiking at Guadalupe Mountains National Park on the Texas–New Mexico border. Located in an out-of-the-way place and totally lacking in tourist facilities (except primitive campgrounds and trails), Guadalupe is a splendid place to escape to. Among our favorite hikes, paralleling one of the few permanent streams in the region, was the McKittrick Canyon trail. Any morning and evening we traveled that way, we met the numerous mule deer that spend summers in the lonely high backcountry but congregate here for the winter. It was a pleasure shooting them with the stark, desert-canyon vegetation, so different from that of the northern Rockies. We also found a good many unwary mule deer at nearby Carlsbad Caverns National Park, which is much better known for its underground caverns and great flights of bats each summer evening at dusk.

Add Mesa Verde National Park in southwestern Colorado to the list of places a wildlife photographer in search of trophies might well explore. Like many other parks, this one is virtually deserted after the aspen leaves fall in September. But some of the best mule bucks we have seen wander down close to park roads that may at times be closed by snow. The muleys are not as confiding here as at Yellowstone, Guadalupe, and the Canadian Rockies parks, but there are some remarkable heads out there waiting for photographers with a little more patience and longer telephoto lenses.

The high rut, which occurs in November almost everywhere, is the period when muleys such as this lip-curling buck best perform for the camera.

Above: Serious photographers are always ready to shoot the pre-rut antics of mule deer. This buck scrapes brush with his antlers and then licks the scraped areas. Facing page: The toughest part about shooting this blizzard photo was keeping the lens glass free of snow.

Almost all the mule deer photos in this book were taken in national parks, national wildlife refuges, and state parks where there are no rifle hunting seasons. Of course it is possible to photograph deer outside sanctuaries, and I admire anyone who does so successfully. The greater the hunting pressure, the more difficult it is to approach mule deer or any other big game. So we naturally concentrate in the protected areas for more certain results. Also, arguably, the deer behave more naturally where people, photographers included, are regarded only as parts of the landscape to be watched, but not to be feared. We believe that only in parks is it worthwhile to invest the long time and energy in hiking on wilderness trails if the goal is locating photographable wildlife.

Park photography, especially in popular parks, does have its drawbacks during the peak of summertime travel. Late one afternoon on Signal Mountain in Wyoming's Grand Teton National Park, we spotted a pair of fine mule bucks in velvet not far from the narrow road that switchbacks to the summit. Even when we pulled off into a parking space to set up cameras (usually a signal that something photographable is nearby), several passing cars paid no attention to us

and failed to see the deer, which were standing in mottled shadow. But the instant the deer walked into open sunlight and we began shooting, a minor traffic jam developed. People jumped out of vehicles, cameras clicked all around us, and videos whirred. And no wonder. What we all saw in our viewfinders was a memorable scene of handsome animals in reddish coats, antlers in velvet, wading flank-deep in wildflowers, seeming unmindful of the human attention. But it ended suddenly when a small busload of teenagers, radios turned on full power, from a nearby church camp arrived. All occupants exploded out of the bus and ran toward the bucks, which also ran and were not seen again in the vicinity until September.

By contrast, the far fewer people a photographer meets beyond the pavements, on hiking trails, are invariably quiet and appreciative of anything they see.

Our technique for photographing mule deer is very simple. We find most of them first by hiking or driving. Years of experience have taught us which areas are most likely to contain animals at different seasons. We spend a lot of time in the field during the annual rut, which takes place in November almost everywhere. At this time the deer are the most active and the least shy,

and offer the most exciting photo opportunities. November is also interesting because its often unsettled weather creates unusual lighting conditions. What begins as a sunny, fairly warm day can end with a sudden snow squall, or vice versa. It isn't always comfortable, but I relish being out in mule deer country in November, and that makes it easier to endure the bad weather.

After locating the deer, we take our time setting up cameras with telephoto lenses and extending the tripod legs. Occasionally the deer are near enough that we need go no farther. But when, as is usually the case, they are farther away, we begin to approach them very slowly, at an angle—never directly. We are always careful to make no sudden motions that might be interpreted as threatening. We do not hide or try to stay out of sight. Hunters may be able to sneak up on mule deer, but a photographer must approach much closer than rifle range, and the senses of mule deer are far too keen for even the best woodsman to reach such a short distance undetected. We make a special effort to remain in view so the mule deer can also keep an eye on us. Most of the time, in this way, they soon accept our presence and we are able to reach reasonable camera range. Often we are able to exchange long telephoto lenses for shorter ones. If our targets show any signs of nervousness, we pause or back away. You cannot shoot acceptable wildlife pictures by frightening or driving your subjects away, and besides it just doesn't seem right. Call it ethics.

Equipment and Gear
Cameras, Tripods, and Film

All of the photographs in this book were taken during the past twenty years with 35mm single lens reflex (SLR) cameras, which are the best for almost any wildlife work. A modern 35mm SLR is light in weight, easy to use, fits well in the hands, is compact and durable, and will (or should) withstand a good bit of rough use. If you are starting from scratch, we advise selecting a 35mm SLR that is part of a system that includes a variety of lenses from close-up to fairly long telephotos. All of our cameras (we carry spares as well as the ones in our hands) are equipped with motor drives (which advance film automatically) and automatic focus. All of this gear is expensive, but for us it's also essential.

We use a variety of lenses, from a 35–80mm zoom for landscapes to a 80–200mm zoom for the least wary animals, to 300mm, 400mm, and 600mm telephoto lenses. The longer lenses are used for most of the mule deer photography. We also carry 1.4X extenders that fit between lens and camera to increase the focal length and power of our telephoto lenses, when very shy animals make it necessary. All of these get heavy use during a year's time.

When using any lenses up to 300mm, I prefer to hand-hold the camera and lens for better mobility and composition. I may sit down and use my elbows propped on my knees as a tripod. Or I may use a large rock or tree trunk for added stability. But with 400mm or 600mm lenses, we use tripods sturdy enough to support their considerable weight. The tripod legs should be individually adjustable for setting up on uneven ground. Although a consensus of wildlife photographers might prefer monoball tripod heads, I much prefer a Wimberley (see address in "Organizations"), which uses pivot mechanisms, and which, although heavier, is vastly smoother and faster to use, especially when shooting wary creatures in action.

Peggy and I work close together, in rich companionship, all the time. We do shoot from somewhat different angles and distances, using lenses of different focal length, to increase our chances of catching some interesting but brief behavior or sudden motion on film.

We use only slide (or positive or -chrome) film, usually slow speed, with an ASA-ISO of 50 to 100 when the light is very bright, and faster film, say ASA-ISO 200, on cloudy or darker days. No single brand of film now manufactured is best for every condition of light that might be encountered day in and day out, at high and low altitudes, summer and winter. So maybe the best photography advice we can give is this: Most of the time, use whatever film seems to give you results that please you most, but interchange your standards with other types from time to time for insurance or for a different way of seeing things.

Vehicles

While hunting the mule deer on these pages, we've found that other equipment has been just as important as the photo gear. For example we travel in a small, self-contained van that is a "hunting camp" wherever we park it. It carries far too much photo gear and also can serve as a photo blind. With the van we can overnight near our subjects, often right among them, and be ready to start shooting soon after dawn, the best time of day. When not near our photo "prey," we stop

Above: Mule deer country is always beautiful. Here, a cold, pure stream flows around a wading buck. Left: This buck has wandered down from high summer range to rest and feed, adding body fat in the period before the rut and wandering into the range of our lenses. Overleaf: Young bucks in the velvet and red summer coats posture and pose in Banff National Park, Alberta.

The sight of a handsome buck like this can lead to buck fever, and even veteran photographers can sprout five thumbs on each hand in the presence of such an animal.

With Five Thumbs

As photographers, we have enjoyed our good days, even our spectacular days, and we have known our disappointments. Thinking of the latter, I recall too well one late summer morning in the Cascade Creek area of Alberta's Banff National Park. My interest this time was in bighorn sheep, rather than deer. With my camera and a 300mm (or six-power) lens among the gear in my backpack, I climbed quickly for an hour or so toward where a herd of eight fine rams, most with fully curled horns, had bedded on a high ridge. I had the rams in sight throughout my climb and since they are fairly accustomed to seeing photographers here, and the day was sunny, I knew this would be a great shoot.

But wildlife photography rarely works that way. By the time I was approaching camera range, on legs that complained about climbing any farther, the sheep suddenly stood up, stretched, and briefly looked at me. Then all followed the leader, which had the heaviest horns in the herd, off the sunny ridge and down into the deep shadow of a ravine, out of sight. I sat down dejected to ponder what to do next. It seemed useless to pursue the sheep.

For several minutes that ridge on top of the world was silent except for my own pulse. Suddenly I heard loose pebbles rolling down the slope behind me. I turned slowly, fearing at first that the pebble roller might be a grizzly. But what I saw instead was a monster mule deer buck staring back at me. It had just stood up from its bed. I swear I could see the puzzlement on its face. I must have been more totally locked on those bighorns than I had realized . . . to pass so close to that mule deer and yet not see it. Unlike the sheep, it watched me rather than move away.

I aimed the camera toward the deer and squeezed off two or three exposures. Then I heard the metallic sound that announced the end of the roll of film had been reached. With five thumbs on each hand, I removed that roll from the camera and fumbled in the backpack for a fresh one. But nothing. I had committed the photographer's cardinal error. I had forgotten to bring extra film. All I could do was sit and watch an outstanding, unafraid mule deer bed down beneath a rock ledge and gaze out over the magnificent Canadian Rockies landscape. It was the first time I had ever made such a serious mistake and, hopefully, fingers crossed, the last.

Facing page: A fine muley buck debates flight versus holding tight and saving energy, unaware that he is posing for a Christmas portrait.

at campgrounds. Located throughout mule deer country of the West, the KOA, or Kampgrounds of America, chain offers secure, pleasant camp sites for the traveling photographer (see address in "Organizations").

Clothing

Proper clothing, especially in the bitter weather toward the end of the mule deer's breeding season, can often make the difference between poor and excellent photo results. Sharp exposures are difficult for a shivering photographer. Build your wardrobe around insulated boots large enough to fit easily over thick socks. The right combination will keep feet warm and dry despite rock-bottom temperatures and deep snow, even when you must stand motionless for long periods of time. Next most important are gloves, light, full-fingered ones that fit inside heavy mittens attached to your sleeves to prevent loss.

Between the gloves and boots, layer your clothing so that you can add or remove shirts, vests, or sweaters as the weather changes. But for extremely cold, even subzero weather, we have found no garments to match those of fine, two-ply worsted wool manufactured by Sleeping Indian Designs in Jackson, Wyoming (see address in "Organizations"). The cap, parka, and pants will long resist rain, but are warm even when wet (which cannot be claimed by down-filled clothing). I have found it possible to kneel or lie down, even wallow, in deep snow to shoot low-angle pictures without the least chilling.

From time to time, backpacks, rucksacks, or beltpacks will be needed by anyone who seriously tracks mule deer with a camera. A poncho for the photographer and a rain hood to cover the camera and lens can come in handy during summer squalls. My favorite gear also includes a baseball cap. It is impossible, or at least unpleasant, to travel far in mule deer country without comfortable boots that are well broken in before you hit the trail. And every summer, the handiest item of all has been the container of insect repellent carried ready to use in a shirt pocket.

Left: Backlighting (with the sun behind the subject) outlines the antlers of a young buck bedded in Montana. Overleaf: During severe winters, deer must plod through deep snow to find enough browse to survive. The deeper the snow, the more energy expended and the lower the survival rate. This group of does trudged past our cameras.

Coaxing the Camera-Shy

One November, Peggy and I returned to Montana from Minnesota where we had been photographing whitetailed deer for our book *Whitetails: Behavior, Ecology, Conservation*. One well-known technique we had used to coax several whitetail bucks into better camera range was rattling two discarded deer antlers together and then scraping the ground with them. When lovesick whitetail males hear this commotion—which should imitate two bucks fighting and promise does in estrus nearby—they often come immediately to the sound to investigate. If the photographer is patient and does not overdo the volume or frequency of rattling, there is often the chance to shoot pictures of

During the rut, rattling discarded antlers together will often attract mule deer bucks into better photo range.

alert, belligerent deer that fill the camera viewfinder.

Home again in Montana, we came across a nervous mule deer buck on a nearby hillside and in a difficult-to-approach spot. That's when I remembered that the whitetail antlers were still in our van, and I decided to try rattling them just as I had for the Minnesota deer. If they worked on whitetails, why not on muleys, too? I tried it. Without hesitation the mule deer trotted toward us for a closer look. We didn't really get good pictures of that one, but the same technique, using the heavier mule deer antlers, has succeeded many times since.Keep in mind, though, that rattling, calling, or the use of any enticement at all, is not permitted in any national park.

Facing page: A picture of health, this muley doe shows no fear of the approaching winter or of a photographer with a telephoto lens. Above: Stalking deer with a camera is a fascinating, challenging, and regularly rewarding outdoor activity year round, which keeps the stalker young at heart.

Left: Early mornings and evenings are not only the best times to spot mule deer in open areas, they also offer the most dramatic photographic light. Above: The rich, yellow light of early morning makes a memorable image of a wild beauty—a young mule deer doe.

Left: A not-very-shy, national park doe approaches for a super—close-up. Above: A calm muley buck basks in the summer sunshine, having become accustomed to the slow-moving photographer kneeling in the grass.

Organizations

BOONE AND CROCKETT CLUB
Old Milwaukee Depot
250 Station Drive
Missoula, MT 59801
(406) 542-1888

BUFFALO BILL HISTORICAL CENTER
P.O. Box 1000
Cody, WY 82414
(307) 587-4771

CANADIAN NATURE FEDERATION
1 Nicholas Street, Suite 520
Ottawa, ON K1N 7B7 Canada
(613) 562-3447

FOUNDATION FOR
NORTH AMERICAN BIG GAME
Box 2710
Woodbridge, VA 22192

KOA, KAMPGROUNDS OF AMERICA
P.O. Box 30558
Billings, MT 59114
(406) 248-7444

LONGHUNTER SOCIETY
P.O. Box 67
Friendship, IN 47021

NORTH AMERICAN SHED HUNTERS CLUB
19790 Dogwood Street NW
Cedar, MN 55011

POPE AND YOUNG CLUB
P.O. Box 548
Chatfield, MN 55923

SAFARI CLUB INTERNATIONAL
4800 West Gates Pass Road
Tucson, AZ 85745

SLEEPING INDIAN DESIGNS
P.O. Box 8517
Jackson, WY 83001
Catalog available: (800) 334-5457

TROPHY WILDLIFE RECORDS
OF BRITISH COLUMBIA
P.O. Box 22
Nanoose, BC V0R 2R0 Canada
(604) 468-7773 or (604) 390-2846

WIMBERLEY DESIGN
133 Bryarly Road
Winchester, VA 22603
(540) 665-2744

References

Bauer, Erwin. *Antlers: Nature's Majestic Crown.* Stillwater, MN: Voyageur Press, 1995.

Bauer, Erwin. *Deer in their World.* New York: Outdoor Life Books, 1983.

Bauer, Erwin. *Horned and Antlered Game.* New York: Outdoor Life Books, 1986.

Bauer, Erwin. *Whitetails: Behavior, Ecology, Conservation.* Stillwater, MN: Voyageur Press, 1993.

Boone and Crockett Club. *Records of North American Big Game.* 10th ed. Missoula, MT, 1993.

Dalrymple, Byron. *North American Big Game Animals.* New York: Outdoor Life Books, 1978.

Putnam, Rory. *The Natural History of Deer.* Ithaca, NY: Cornell University Press, 1988.

Rue, Leonard Lee III. *The Deer of North America.* Harrisburg, PA: Stackpole, 1956.

Seton, Ernest T. *Lives of Game Animals.* New York: Literary Guild of America, 1937.

Strickland, D. *Mule Deer of the Medicine Bow Mountains.* Cheyenne, WY: Wyoming Fish and Game Department, 1975.

Taylor, Walter P., editor. *The Deer of North America.* Harrisburg, PA: Stackpole, 1956.

Whitehead, G. Kenneth. *Deer of the World.* New York: Viking Press, 1972.

Whitehead, G. Kenneth. *The Whitehead Encyclopedia of Deer.* Stillwater, MN: Voyageur Press, 1993.

Wyoming Fish and Game Department. *Mule Deer of Wyoming.* Cheyenne, WY, 1975.

Index

About the Bauers

Erwin and Peggy Bauer are busy, full-time photographers and writers of travel, adventure, and environmental subjects. Based in Paradise Valley, Montana, the Bauers have specialized in photographing wildlife worldwide for over forty years. Their images come from the Arctic to the Antarctic, Borneo to Brazil, Africa to India, Madagascar to Malaysia, and beyond.

Erwin and Peggy Bauer may be the most frequently published wildlife photographers in the world today. The Bauers' recent magazine credits include *Natural History, Outdoor Life, Audubon, National Geographic,* *Smithsonian, Wildlife Conservation, National Wildlife* and *International Wildlife, Sierra, Safari, Chevron USA,* and *Nature Conservancy.* Their photographs annually illustrate the calendars of Voyageur Press, the Sierra Club, the Audubon Society, World Wildlife Fund, and others. The Bauers have more than a dozen books currently in print, including *Yellowstone, Whitetails,* and *Antlers: Nature's Majestic Crown,* all three published by Voyageur Press. The couple has won many awards for wildlife photography in national and international photographic competitions.